The Buzz

Creating a Thriving and Collaborative Staff Learning Culture

Tracey Ezard

2015

Copyright © 2015 Tracey Ezard

www.traceyezard.com

All rights reserved. This book or any portion thereof may not be reproduced or used in any manner whatsoever without the express written permission of the publisher except for the use of brief quotations in a book review or scholarly journal.

ISBN: 978-0-6487931-0-6

Tracey Ezard
PO Box 484 Canterbury
Victoria 3126

Cover design by Matt Emery

Illustrations by Tracey Ezard

For Conor and Layla

Thank you for showing me daily what a love of learning,
joy for life and growth mindset look like.

Contents

INTRODUCTION — 1

1. WHAT'S THE BUZZ? — 5

2. BUILDING THE BUZZ — 23

3. GROWTH MINDSET — 35

4. COMPELLING ENVIRONMENT — 61

5. AUTHENTIC DIALOGUE — 97

6. A FINAL REFLECTION — 115

TRACEY'S PROFESSIONAL LEARNING BELIEFS — 119

INTRODUCTION

What are the biggest questions keeping you as an educational leader awake at night? Is it which programs to implement in the school to improve learning outcomes for your students? Is it ways to deal with the daunting amount of welfare and social issues walking in with the students you educate and care for? Is it thinking about how you'll communicate a new direction for the school? Perhaps the most pressing issue is having the resources to run the programs imperative to providing the type of education you wish to provide? Then there are myriad parent issues, behaviour issues, staff issues, bureaucracy, paperwork ... the list goes on and on. The tossing and turning in bed continues and our heads are full of what to do and how to do it.

But the biggest question worrying many leaders embarking on the journey of creating a great school is:

How do I move my staff?

Let's face it — we are creatures of habit. We can get stuck doing the same thing over and over and become comfortable doing that. Changing and/or moving on goes against our innate need for safety. Many of us like comfortable. Too much change can be stressful and just plain annoying. Why can't things just stay the same? Why the constant pressure to keep moving?

Yet the changing context of the world and education means we can't stay comfortable. We need to be constantly improving. We need to apply what we know now to unknown future tasks. We need savvy, forward-thinking, brave educators who are not afraid to trial new ways of approaching teaching and make their own learning a key pillar of their work. These people are true learners themselves. They are agile in their learning and respond to the needs of their students fluidly and flexibly. We need teachers who see that true collaboration and learning with peers reaps huge rewards for the students they teach, through better teaching and learning, higher levels of engagement and more focus on the student as an individual.

Staff motivation doesn't have to be complex. In fact, it's pretty simple. You just need to tap into people's passion for teaching and making a difference, which is a big driver for most teachers. I haven't met a teacher yet who doesn't want to do the very best they can. If you can build a professional learning community that thrives on its challenges and achievements and is always in a state of growth, the outcomes for students are high.

The job for leaders is to tap into this passion and drive in a way that builds momentum – a buzz. The buzz is based on the intersection and development of three aspects – mindset, environment and dialogue. Mindset is about growth and possibility. Environment must be compelling for professionals to collaborate and learn together. Dialogue challenges and engages people in proactive and supported growth. We have to move our thinking to one of agility and growth, rather than stability and constancy. No longer is it acceptable to teach the same things in the same way we taught them 10 or 20 years ago.

The new world our students are a part of will demand more of them than any other generation. They will have 24-hour access to information and lots of it. More of them will work in jobs that require creative, analytical and innovative thinking rather than grunt and mechanical labour. They are part of a generation that connects and learns virtually as well as in person and sees technology as simply the way the world is – not an add on. As digital natives, they are more globally connected. The world is becoming smaller for all of us with distance not a barrier to work or learning options.

Futurists speak of prospective jobs continuing to move into the innovation and disruption space, with technology as the centerpiece. Entrepreneurial thinking that hacks through the cumbersome ways we have always done things is rising to the fore, with clever, out-of-the-box solutions to well-worn problems we have battled to solve. For example, using the software tool Evernote I can put all my thoughts, photos, documents, links, reminders, etc. into the one program that is accessible from all of my devices and saves me having to drag everything around with me.

Social entrepreneurship is also on the rise with people, including youth, creating businesses that support and give back to the community rather than simply making profit from it.

Our health and welfare needs will continue to grow, with the next generation carrying the burden of caring for a society that, even with advances in healthcare, is more sedentary and overweight, and has more complex medical conditions than at any other time in history.

How do we keep abreast of all of this in the school context?

INTRODUCTION

By being agile and responsive educators, and by creating thriving professional learning cultures that inspire us to trial, test and evaluate new ways of teaching and new ways of learning. These people and places have a buzz and I want to share the recipe with you.

As both an educational leader in the state system and an educational consultant and facilitator in government, private and catholic sectors I have been immersed in professional learning communities for the whole of my career. *The Buzz* is based on my observations, learning, thinking, and reflection on and with professional educators I have worked with over 25 years.

There is growing research on the need for strong professional learning communities within schools to encourage reflection and change practice. *The Buzz* provides a practical approach to building a school's professional learning community. How do we build trust? How do we create a culture of collaboration? *The Buzz* examines the foundational thinking that we internally experience when our practice is being put under the microscope and we expose ourselves and our vulnerabilities to learn and grow with our colleagues.

HOW TO USE THIS BOOK

This book is designed to give the educational leader a lens to put over his or her own professional learning environment and see where traction and momentum can be built to create the buzz.

The first section of the book (chapters 1 and 2) provides you with the architecture of the buzz — something I call *learning intelligence*. This section provides the context for building a culture of collaboration and trust.

The second section of the book (chapters 3 to 5) is full of ways to identify your position on the path of creating this thriving learning environment, and offers key activities and approaches develop it further. The approaches move between things you can apply yourself to make sure you are priming yourself as a leader of the buzz, and things to reflect on and do as a team or whole school.

Within *The Buzz* visual images and models spark the brain. This is the way I work as a graphic facilitator — creating visuals to lend weight to the words.

1. WHAT'S THE BUZZ?

LEARNING INTELLIGENCE a.k.a THE BUZZ

Ever been in a situation that changed the way you see the world? It may not have seemed profound at the time, but upon reflection it urged a real shift in your thinking.

When I was in my third year of teaching, I met Steven. He was a smart, savvy and cheeky Year 5 student. He was clever, but found school boring and constricting. Teachers were the bane of his life and he showed it by acting up in all sorts of ways. He knew every teacher's 'hot buttons' and didn't hesitate to use them when he felt like it. I didn't teach Steven directly, but had him in some small-group work for various activities, such as gifted and talented programs or musical productions. Usually I loved him. He was the type of kid who was suggesting, 'Stay on your toes – I'm worth the hard work getting through to me. If you do, I'll give you all I've got'. So he and I had a pretty good relationship. I loved the way he thought and his push-the-boundaries attitude.

One day, though, his usual button-pushing got the better of me. He looked at me and said with delight: 'I'm making you grit your teeth'. And he was right, the little so and so! He knew, before I was consciously aware, that I was reacting to him in a less-than-useful way.

That day I switched on to the need to be more in tune to my resourcefulness and learn better ways to manage myself when stressed, tired or overwhelmed. Not only that, it set me on a road to find out more about emotional intelligence and skills that make us more emotionally aware of ourselves and others. It's okay just to learn something – just gain the information and say, 'Yes I know that' but I wanted to live the learning. Really test it, play with it, embed it.

I'm happy to say that I am still playing with the same essential question: **How can we be our most resourceful in our work?** How can we be in a state that always brings the best of ourselves to the situation with enough resources at our disposal?

Every day I'm learning more and more about that through reading, professional learning, listening to experts, looking at theories. I make sure I hang out with people who stretch my thinking and encourage me to grow. Best of all I get to learn from the people I work with every day. They are constantly giving me new ideas and approaches to try. Some (many) of the ideas fail. That's okay because failing is part of learning and I know that *learning intelligence*, the ability to apply, synthesise, evaluate, discard or embed, is a growing intelligence. It's never static. Learning intelligence helps me to be an agile and adaptive learner

The most important element of learning intelligence is the mindset of curiosity and growth. Even in the darkest of environments and the darkest conversations, someone with a strong sense of learning intelligence can pull themselves out with a good dose of 'I wonder'. They see possibility. They ask 'what if?'.

To start my business working in developing leaders, I drew on my experience in teaching and in leadership positions in education and business as well as my areas of study. The main focus of my work was in developing emotional intelligence, resourcefulness and wellbeing.

Pivotal to high emotional intelligence is understanding the mindset, values and beliefs that drive behaviour. These beliefs shape who we are as individuals and as team players and collaborators.

After a number of years it became increasingly important for me to connect the work I was doing with a school's or organisation's leaders with the strategic direction of that school or organisation. No longer did it seem feasible to work with leaders on growing themselves and their teams without a strong link to what they were doing and where they were going.

As soon as I branched out into the strategy area something else became very evident. Schools with a thriving professional learning community – with a buzz – were able to collaborate on their strategic work much more effectively. People took responsibility and accountability for their part of the work and for their own learning. They could have robust debate about what needed to happen to get the student outcomes they were after, and they put together plans to make it happen. More and more I began to see that not only do we need to build our ability to emotionally manage ourselves and others (emotional intelligence) and our strategic thinking, but we also need to build our ability to learn as adults in a fearless, curious and adventurous way.

Working with many school leaders and teachers over the past 10 years I have observed that leaders who get the most traction are those who are voracious learners themselves. Not just academic learning, but deeply embedded, tested, trialed, reflective learning from experiences.

The application of learning and reflection on our own performance as adults is always fraught with danger. We have deeply embedded beliefs and assumptions about our skills, capabilities and limitations — our thoughts about right and wrong and whether something fits our view of the world. Couple this with fear of failure, over-use of comparison and occasional power issues and the outlook can be bleak. Yet deep personal learning and growth as an educator and professional can also be one of the most transformative and satisfying journeys.

Optimism and possibility, risks and possible failures, are part of the journey.

In schools our own learning is pivotal to the success of the students. If educators do not see learning as a personal cornerstone of their work, then why should anyone else? The development of a school's professional learning environment is a key element of any thriving school's culture.

Collective wisdom and building collective capacity are the way of the future. We need to be creating this within our staff learning community or the future will pass us by.

Getting a good sense of how strong our buzz is (is it a buzz, just a hum or are those just crickets chirping?) can be a challenge when you're sitting in the middle of it. To gauge what is going on we need to sit back and reflect on ourselves and the school. The metaphor of the balcony and the dance floor, coined by Ronald Heifetz and Marty Linsky in *Leadership on the Line*, is a useful mindset to apply here.

The balcony and dance floor refers to the ability to look at the situation, organisation and interaction from a balcony view, where we can make more objective evaluation and analysis of what is going on and what is needed. When we are down on the dance floor, we can be swamped with day-to-day tasks and not see past our noses.

The balcony can be used in a very strategic way to ask: Where are our challenges and strengths? Where are we headed? What are our strategies? It can be used in a very personal, reflective way: If I replay that conversation or that meeting from a balcony viewpoint, what can I learn from it? Can I gain more insight into what occurred? Do I see another way I might have addressed the situation? The balcony can also be used as a metaphoric pause, when you stop momentarily to work out your next step, based on a different perspective from the present moment.

As you read this book I encourage you to use the ideas put forward as a lens through which to look at the dance floor of your learning culture. Make sure you get good objective data about what is really happening and don't make plans that are only informed by a distant balcony view. While the balcony view offers an important perspective, be careful not to make plans that are only informed by this view. To find out what is really occurring, talk with the people involved and understand their perspectives and drivers. Be pragmatic and inspirational about co-creating the thriving and collaborative culture you're after. Schools that buzz with that kind of culture have learning intelligence.

Learning intelligence needs to be evident at three levels for a school to create a truly thriving professional learning culture. These three levels are like the layers of an onion. In the centre is the individual, the strength of learning intelligence in each individual member affects the quality of the outer layers. The middle layer represents all the teams within the school structure and the way they work together. The outer layer is the school unit as a complete, thriving learning organisation. If one of these levels is not pulling its weight with regard to learning, the outcomes are not as strong, which can lead to frustration for many.

Of course each school is also a part of a greater system, which can be viewed as a wider learning community. Schools can contribute to this community by linking and learning with other schools. Some innovative and clever schools go further by linking with other parts of the system, such as human services, health professionals and the justice system to create a more effective whole that can provide greater integration to deal with 'wicked' problems like mental health issues, generational poverty, domestic violence, and drug and alcohol issues. Wicked problems refer to problems that are hard to define. There are usually incomplete or contradictory parts to the problem, many changing contexts and requirements. Because the problem 'belongs' to more than one agency, it's often not dealt with correctly or thoroughly. It can be too easily either brushed aside or the responsibility shifts from one group to another without traction.

Even though this system thinking requires schools to look outside themselves to produce change, the ability to create a thriving learning environment and culture within is still the first step.

The Learning Intelligent Self

History was made in November 2014 when, after a 10-year, six-billion-kilometre journey, the *Philae* lander was rocketed from the Rosetta spacecraft and landed on a spinning comet hurtling through space at 18 kilometres per second.

While it's hard for our brains to comprehend the numbers, how amazing to think of the constant feedback and adaption required leading up to that bouncing landing. The evolution in technology since *Rosetta* was initially launched in February 2004 boggles the mind. Imagine the forethought scientists had to create something so far into the future that can still be responsive and adapt to a huge amount of unforeseen scenarios in space, as well as changing technology on Earth. Not only that, but because of the huge distance from Earth, communication from *Rosetta* to the controllers was 28 minutes behind real time!

Learning intelligence is like this mission – crucial information and insights are around us all the time to learn from and adapt or reinforce our approach. We need to be agile and responsive to do this adaption.

As educators our main subjects are human beings – constantly evolving, endlessly changing, learning, responding and growing – so if our approach does not contain these same elements we are going to miss the comet landing every time.

In his study 'Visible Learning' Professor John Hattie researched the things teachers do that have the most effect on learning. Not surprisingly, he found that feedback had a high level of influence. According to Hattie the most powerful feedback is that given from the student to the teacher. It makes learning visible and allows the agile teacher to plan the next steps. Educators who respond to the feedback they receive from learners about whether they are actually learning and use that feedback to inform future learning and teaching strategies are increasing the opportunity for student success. To be able to take on this feedback and access it in a deep and meaningful way, we **must** be in a learning mode ourselves – open, growth orientated and comfortable with an agile approach. We also need to be happy with not being *right* all the time. Then we are using our learning intelligence.

Hattie's book, *Making Learning Visible*, is a valuable resource for focusing teachers on being responsive to feedback and for understanding the factors that can make the biggest impact on learning. This feedback creates a strong second-position opportunity, that is: I see learning not from *my eyes*, but from the eyes of my students. When we are firmly in 'first' position (or 'I') we have a tendency to only see feedback from our own perspective.

My daughter's friend gave me a great example of this when we were talking about her language classes. She is in primary school and has a 50-minute language session each week. Her comment was: 'We just get started on something and then the very next session we are on to something else – I feel like I don't really get a chance to learn it properly before we've moved on.' Even though this is a broad comment, it gives an interesting view of perspective from a student voice.

Great professional learners have a deep-seated drive to bring the best of themselves to school each day. Every time they are in the classroom with students, in conversation with colleagues, parents or other professionals, or simply planning their teaching approach for certain students, their learning intelligence is being used.

Teaching is no longer a one-way street of information, facts and authoritarian insights. Effective teaching relies on continuous feedback loops, reflection and shifts in approach. If we don't see the process of teaching as a robust two-way learning process we are doomed to forever to 'do what we have always done' and not respond to the changing needs of our students.

In the following chapters we will explore how this learning intelligence is manifested – through mindset, environment and dialogue. How crucial is every single member of your staff in creating this? The need for all staff to be totally invested in learners is a critical link to positive outcomes for students. A review of literature by Professor Helen Timperley showed that participation in both professional learning *and* strong observation/feedback loops has a sizeable impact on student outcomes.

 ## The Learning Intelligent Team

Working across a variety of sectors – health, government and business – I see first hand how well we are progressing in utilising teams effectively in education compared to other areas. Smart school leaders and teachers are tuned into the need for high-functioning teams that work well together, and many leaders spend a great amount of time at the end of each school year making sure that the combination of teachers in a team is going to work.

In reality, teamwork, collaborative approaches to learning and implementing new teaching and learning practices are tricky to get right. Getting clarity on the way the team needs to work, the expectations within the team and the goals the team is working on are often topics left off team meeting agendas. There is often a much-used cry of: 'We don't have time to spend on that stuff'. This means teams launch into the year, term or semester without a clear picture of what they need to be working on and how they are going to do it.

The bedrock of a high-functioning team in a school is their ability to learn from themselves and to create an environment of high challenge, high support. Processes that allow for open and robust dialogue within the team are crucial tools. As educators we have so many thinking tools at our fingertips that we use with students – clever ways to think differently, think clearly or explore issues with purpose.

Too often, though, we leave this kind of discussion off the agenda and we stick to the way we've always done it – a list of administrivia that must be talked through endlessly, leaving the important exploration and learning part of the meeting until 'next time'. The environment section of this book will help you focus on your team processes and assist you in fine-tuning the way you think about your precious time together as a team.

 **The Learning Intelligent School: The Buzz**

The great Australian classic film *The Castle* is about a David and Goliath struggle between a working-class family and an airport corporation. It added to our lexicon a fabulous term, 'it's the vibe', which was uttered by the family's vague, seemingly slightly drunk lawyer. He was trying to capture the feeling of the main character's home right next to the main runway of Melbourne's airport ... the atmosphere and energy that was in this family home and how much it meant to its occupants. He had trouble articulating what that feeling was, so settled on talking about 'the vibe'. The vibe is something that many people pick up as soon as they enter a space.

As with many educators visiting schools, my 'cultural antennae' is always up when I walk into a school. I've spent a number of years intent on identifying what it is that makes up the buzz or culture of a school where there are great things happening – a.k.a. the vibe. To help me – and the school staff if they're involved – unpack what can seem to be indefinable, I often use the model created by Carolyn Taylor, which is outlined in her book *Walking the Talk*. Taylor is one of the foremost experts on corporate culture and works with organisations to ensure alignment between what they say and what they do.

Taylor's model gives a great framework to observe, dissect and identify culture. At the base, the very foundation of this model, are the values and beliefs upon which all else is built. These are not the values that often thrown around as being 'our values' but never seen in evidence. You may have witnessed this in stores where the marketing spruiks 'customer service' being their core value, yet they don't have enough staff to cover busy periods or they don't train staff to a high quality to meet the customers' needs. Taylor's model talks about the values that are *really* at play, found through behaviours, systems and symbols. These values are exhibited through three pillars: culture behaviours, culture systems and culture symbols.

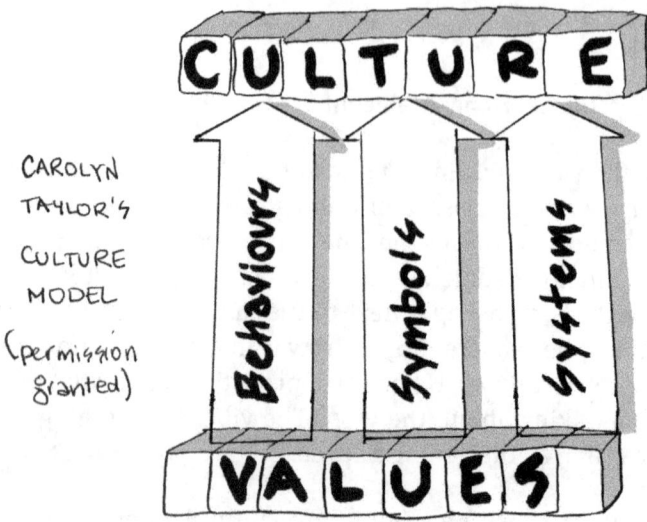

Figure 1 – Culture Model- Carolyn Taylor

Culture Behaviours

The first pillar of behaviour is about the people of influence in your organisation. How do they act out the values that you want as your bedrock? These people are not just the nominated leaders, but people who are the influencers in the staff. They represent the norms of behaviour in your culture. When one of my clients, Jo, became the head of her school, she spent an entire year getting people to say hello to each other in the morning – because no one did! She believed that a welcoming culture was vital to move towards changing the way they had always worked, and this was the behaviour she focused on changing first. Previously, they were not valuing each other as colleagues, as students of the school or as parents. As colleagues, the staff did not see themselves as needing to learn from each other, implying through their actions that others couldn't possibly offer them anything they didn't already know themselves.

This step of expecting people to be more than civil, to be welcoming in their behaviours, was her first step in cracking a culture that appeared aloof, fixed and slightly arrogant. Jo's vision was for a welcoming, community-minded school environment and professional learning culture. This may seem like a small thing, yet the expectation raised the community's awareness about how they were behaving and what they were really valuing.

Culture Systems

The right hand pillar of Carolyn Taylor's model is the hardware, or systems – the timetables, resourcing, staffing, classroom structure, faculty and team structure. These must support the culture. Many schools got clever a long time ago, changing timetables so that teams could have preparation time together to increase collaboration. Flexible learning environments increasingly found in primary schools are examples of systems designed to facilitate the type of teaching, learning and culture that schools know will get better outcomes for students. Agendas and the way team and staff meetings are conducted are also great indicators of culture and of the values being displayed.

Staffroom behaviour can be strongly affected by decisions we make around systems. For example, the crucial question of who should be seated together? What if we have no control over where our teachers do their prep work and they are completely isolated from their team members due to the facility set up? These challenges need to be considered and dealt with if we want a committed and collaborative culture — one with a buzz.

I know of a school that many years ago spent time and money creating great 'caves' for their teams. They had their own jugs, toasters and microwaves in completely separate parts of the school. Teams felt safe and connected in their own areas. Unfortunately, there were not many systems put in place to keep the cross-team connections going. People didn't really have any reason – either socially or professionally – to congregate in the main staff space except for a daily 10 minutes in the morning, where the principal spoke about administrivia. Everyone listened – bored or angry, frustrated or uninterested, then went on their way. The areas were a great systemic move for the teams, but in the end simply caused a great divide when the leaders needed to do some real shifting in terms of teaching and learning. When the expectations to work differently were turned up, the teams bunkered down in their rooms and moaned and complained about whatever was happening to them outside that room. How was morale in that school? ... I'm sure you've guessed. How were results and enrolments? ... Sliding downward.

We can't enable a thriving learning environment in our professional community if we don't provide the systems to help. Often it is the systems that stymie great intentions. Stuck with processes and systems that are out of date and simply tradition ('I've always taught Year 6' or ' I always take the Advanced English Year 8 Class'), we flail around wondering why we are not getting shift. Bold, fearless leaders know that systems need to be shaken up and sometimes tossed out to make a difference to culture.

Culture Symbols

Taylor's central pillar is particularly fascinating. It can be quite hard to identify the symbols of our own culture. We are a bit like the frog in boiling water – we're too close to it to identify our behaviours and systems, which are very symbolic of our culture. Taylor describes the symbols of an organisation as the things that time, money and effort are spent on. Symbols also encompass the rituals that are held dear.

Schools are full of these great rituals – they are the traditions that the students, staff and community often hold onto fiercely. The special way you run assemblies, the songs you sing, award nights, fetes and school productions are obvious symbols of a school. While many of these symbols are things that create the fabric of the school and its community, sometimes the things we hold symbolically dear are not serving us well any more. You may have been instrumental in having to gently prise people from these traditions. A good example would be the major change process you make to ensure that excursions held in your school actually relate to the curriculum, rather than simply be an enjoyable outing to a local farm to watch sheep shearing that's never referred to in class except for some diary entries and artwork of fluffy cotton-ball sheep around the classroom. Prior to the change, it was held on to because it was something 'the kids love and we have gone there for years in Term 3'.

Less obvious are the way you do things, which can be symbolic. At the school where I was assistant principal in Melbourne, we used to farewell any staff leaving by putting together a large book for them. Every teacher had to come up with his or her own page for the person leaving. The contributions were always full of songs that 'roasted' the person or photos with humorous messages. One of our beloved staff, Liz, was responsible for reading them out to the staff member in question in front of everyone at a morning tea. She would put on a great show and amp it up. It was always great fun and very symbolic of the camaraderie at the school. Everyone genuinely cared for everyone else and this was one of the traditions or symbolic acts to show it.

Symbols are the stories told by us and others about our school. The barbecue conversation about the school when teachers or parents get together is a great way to pick up the symbols. 'At my school we …'. These are the behaviours or systems that are now so important they take on legendary status.

Symbols can occur in simple everyday acts: the call from the principal to the parent to let them know about something fabulous their child has done; the way new staff and students in the school are welcomed by everyone; the way the timetable is created so teachers have time to plan together; the provision of furniture that provides a flexible learning space.

In terms of learning intelligence, this book is full of examples symbolic of a thriving professional learning culture. But when considering the symbols of this culture we also need to analyse the symbols of our leadership in this space. Do you attend professional learning with your staff? Do you discuss the impact in the classroom and beyond? Do you create the same rigour and reflective practice in your leadership team that you want in your teachers? Do you set the environment and model the learning behaviours to others?

A great learning culture isn't just nice to have. It has real and tangible impact on the effectiveness of teachers and the quality of the teaching. Professor Helen Timperley found that: 'Teachers working in schools with more supportive professional environments continued to improve significantly after three years, while teachers in the least supportive schools actually declined in their effectiveness.'

What are the symbols in your school that reflect the strength of your collective learning intelligence? Do they suggest it is thriving and that you are fanning those flames?

Beyond our own Grounds

Schools that have mastered learning intelligence often show strong collegiate support to other schools and organisations, sharing their learning beyond the boundaries of their own educational space. When learning and supporting each other is embedded in the fabric of the school, it is inevitable that this philosophy spills out of the school and into the collegiate connections between schools, through teaching and learning networks and principal networks.

There are some places where this is not the case and the focus of the education staff is competitive and knowledge-keeping not knowledge-sharing. In these schools a true growth mindset doesn't exist. A growth mindset is focused on abundance. Abundance facilitates the purpose of education, which is to create great learning environments for all students, no matter where they go to school.

KEY ELEMENTS OF THE BUZZ: MINDSET, ENVIRONMENT, DIALOGUE

Element #1
Build a Growth Mindset

At its base the culture of a learning organisation springs from the beliefs held by the individuals within, most importantly by those of influence. Clarifying what growth really looks like and the internal approach we need to take to tackle challenges, obstacles and change is key to developing culture. Growth behaviours come from growth beliefs. Growth beliefs are about forward action and internal responsibility to learning. When we move to action, we attempt new things, tackle obstacles and persist with challenges. Growth beliefs help people see obstacles and challenges as opportunities to be flexible and adaptable.

As a team, setting clear outcomes and purpose allows us to collaborate on finding the way forward. In terms of mindset, articulating where we are heading can give certainty. When we set our intention and the outcomes we are looking for, we seed the movement towards it. It gives us internal clarity. We can start to co-create and collaborate, or simply experiment, learning along the way, gaining momentum through commitment towards it happening. It also gives us the opportunity to really see if we have alignment between what we are thinking and how we believe we are going to achieve it.

When the mindset is about growth and possibility and there is clarity of outcomes, shift becomes easier. The learning mindset develops in people so that different perspectives are accessed as a part of the process. We start to reframe tricky situations and major change internally as well as externally, allowing for possibility – rather than impossibility – to drive our decisions.

Being able to reframe is a critical part of learning intelligence. Reframing means to express or think about a concept or issue differently. Reframing can disrupt our habitual ways of thinking about something. Effective reframing can help people see the positive slant to something that was previously seen as a negative. Sometimes we just need a little jolt to guide us to look at the subject differently.

When I was touring a potential school for my second child's secondary education, I was really impressed with the quiet, focused buzz of the whole place. Students were either working individually on laptops or in discussion groups. Others were interacting with each other to get a hands-on project happening. The teachers were not obvious (I had to search them out), they were explaining something to a small group or working one-on-one with individuals. Students were moving around to the area they needed quietly and purposefully.

The principal had left all the parents on the tour with a bunch of students so we could ask any questions we wanted of them. One of parents said: 'There is such a great sense of calm, energy in the school, everyone working purposefully and enjoying it by the looks of it. Can you tell me what you think helps this?' The students gave their thoughts, and then one said, 'And we have a "No Yell" policy'.

Ah – said the educator in me – so the students have clear behaviour expectations. The student went on to say: 'The teachers are not permitted to raise their voices with us, and if they do we are able to raise the issue with the principal or assistant principals.' I laughed, reflecting the great assumption had just been reframed for me. I had *assumed* that the policy was all about student behavior protocols. It also gave me deeper insight into some of the beliefs the school is being built on – mutual respect and student voice.

Innovation comes from reframing our core beliefs into seeing other options and ways of thinking.

Element # 2
Create a Compelling Environment

A connectedness happens in an environment when people are learning together. It is not visible, yet it can be felt if we have our radars out. This connectedness contributes to the buzz. It's based on trust and a willingness to collaborate and grow together. We need to create compelling spaces in schools for learning, collaboration and exploration. This space takes in not only the physical set-up of rooms and meetings, but also the energy that is created.

Creating a compelling environment is also about strategically using processes that enable exploration of the challenges, strengths, context and possibilities. As leaders we need to lead, facilitate and contribute to these discussions skillfully, ensuring we are not afraid of divergence of opinion. Divergence of opinion is a vital part of robust problem solving and a thriving learning environment. Carefully chosen processes and tools can move this divergent discussion into convergence around options, proposed strategies and actions.

Rich debate about our school requires us to get over seeing feedback as conflict. A compelling environment is all about being able to have these conversations in a positive and exploratory frame – one of inquiry rather than right and wrong.

A thriving environment for learning is also about using a variety of ways to activate adult learning. We do this for students but not so much for ourselves. We tend to use too much auditory – one person speaking, everyone else listening. Yawn …

Great learning cultures don't spend precious time talking *at* people. To gain traction and engage people in the forward direction of the school, we need to provide opportunities for learning through a whole range of strategies.

The Compelling Environment chapter 4 of the book gives you a number of tools to mix up professional learning interactions – from staff meetings and team meetings through to specific professional learning sessions. Compelling environments not only assist our learning, they help us become more agile in our thinking.

Element # 3
Have Authentic Dialogue

Dialogue that is rich and fruitful is the third foundational element to creating the buzz. In buzzy environments, robust conversations about teaching and learning are the norm. People feel supported to state their opinions and these opinions are valued. Diversity of opinion is seen as a core element to finding the right path. Most importantly, people are OK with giving and receiving feedback about their own development and see it as a critical part of their growth. Outside of an authentic dialogue mindset, feedback is something many people struggle with.

These conversations build trust. By contrast, any interaction where trust in intention is low is a recipe for disaster. People warily approach the discussion, protecting themselves from vulnerability and putting up defensive shields.

Authentic dialogue is essentially about building trust and connection – then the real work and collaboration can begin. Dialogue that is authentically about the work, about learning and about continually improving, is dependent on the work we have done in setting up a growth mindset and the environment. These elements create the recipe for purposeful and fruitful discussion.

By having greater clarity of outcomes and vision, and the right tools and processes to enable the discussions, the dialogue becomes congruent and authentic. We spend less time on blame and justifications. People are keen to be proactive and work together to make real change in teaching and learning. Authentic dialogue takes mindfulness and time. But even when we are busy we can create an environment of dialogue rather than simply telling. The default – especially when busy – is: *I speak at you. You listen. You nod and say yes. You go away and do it.* When it comes to dialogue we need to reflect on how the majority of our time is spent. If we are always in 'telling mode' then things need to change. One-way communication doesn't create momentum and certainly won't help create intrinsic motivation in staff. In fact, it can move staff either to a place of rebellion or victim.

Great leaders ask great questions that help bring about new thinking, not the same thinking. Think about your own practice. What are some great questions you've asked your team recently that have opened up a whole new way of looking at something?

To help people shift their thinking ask explorative and generative questions.

2. BUILDING THE BUZZ

SHIFTING TO THE BUZZ

One important aspect of leading is finding ways to shift the status quo to make sure the school is evolving, not stuck in a comfort zone. For me, leadership is about movement. Only then are we propelled forward into our learning zone – where growth, problem solving and creativity are found.

The start-up period of experimentation and learning is followed by a time of growth and development. Inevitably, however, every curve turns downward. The chapters ahead provide a framework and practical applications for building the learning intelligence of your school and encouraging the curve upward. This will help you gain committed collaboration from your staff to realise your school's potential.

Figure 2: The 6 Stages to the Buzz is a model I have developed through my work with schools. It charts a school's journey towards creating a collaborative, engaged environment of growth. Not every school starts at the danger zone, and different schools progress through these stages at different paces, but this model is a useful tool to identify what place your school is in and how to move forward from it.

Focusing on building a thriving collaborative learning environment will help you keep above the line, that is, out of the danger zone of corrosion and complacency. Helping your leaders and staff engage in the purpose and intent of the school through meaningful activities aimed at moving up the ladder towards the buzz will provide traction for growth and transformation.

In essence, leaders of thriving collaborative school environments are passionate about the need for a co-created vision and set of beliefs that help align staff with purpose. They also encourage strong debate to shape strategic actions and an environment where people can work together. The end game is the students – the individual and the collective – receiving the best education possible. The best education is at the core of these visions, and the strategies and culture that fall out of them.

THE 6 STAGES TO THE BUZZ

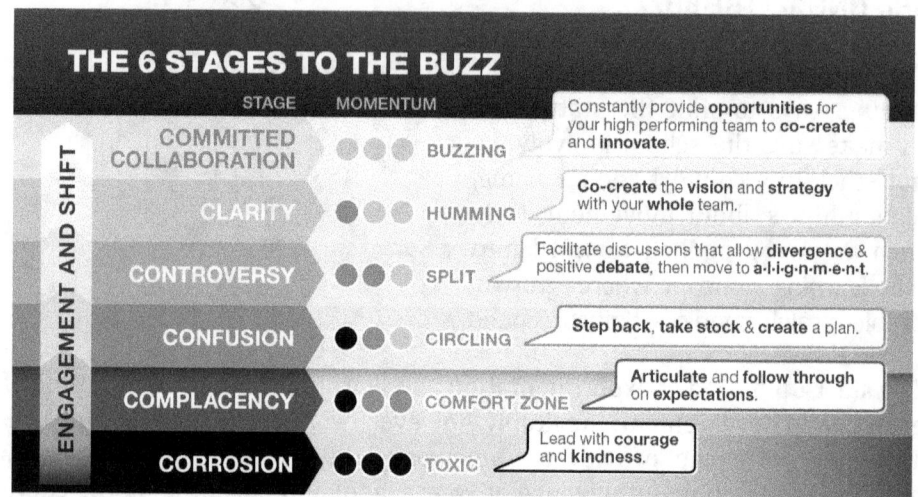

Figure 2 – The 6 Stages to the Buzz

What place is your school in now?

1. Corrosion

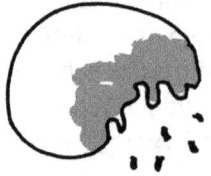

The bottom rung of the ladder is the corrosive level. The definition of corrosion: *The gradual destruction of materials by chemical reaction with their environment.*

Have you ever walked into an environment that felt toxic? You can feel it in the air. People tend not to even look at or acknowledge each other. There seems to be no trust – in fact there is often a strong sense of distrust.

A corrosive work environment is the home of the toxic workplace. In this space people of influence seem to be committed to creating an environment of fear and anxiety. In reality they may not even be aware they are doing it; their self-awareness may be low and/or they do not have much empathy for others. Some may be fearful themselves so their behaviours are those of 'survival of the fittest'. Whatever the underlying reasons, something major has to shift and only strong leadership will bring a school out of this stage.

This stage can be an indicator of past ineffective leadership. Some behaviours exhibited may be entrenched unconscious techniques remnant of a leadership regime that was authoritarian, fear based and not conducive to a thriving environment. People then learn the behaviours of survival.

Following are some of the hallmarks of the corrosive environment.

Fear

When fear is present, there is a genuine feeling of insecurity for many people on staff. They are afraid to speak their mind or voice their concerns. Fear also stands as a big barrier to active experimentation and evaluation of new approaches in teaching and learning. There is just too much to lose with regard to personal safety and wellbeing. It's easier to stay with the status quo or retreat.

Unprofessional behaviour

Unchecked, unprofessional behaviour runs rife and is often normalised. People behave in inappropriate ways, but little has ever been done to address the behaviours or set clear expectations about what should be happening. There is little or no follow-up to underperformance. Professional standards are not articulated, supported or embedded into the culture. When a school is in this corrosive space quite often people do want it to be different; they are just too scared to speak up about it.

Feedback = conflict

During the corrosive stage any feedback around shifting behaviour, approach or perspectives is taken as personal attack. In my experience, this is one of the biggest hurdles to get through as a leader. Co-creating an environment of trust and collaboration, where people see feedback as a vital part of growth, appears a long way in the distance.

Lack of vision and innovation

The dreams and visions of the school are far from people's realities and there is a distinct lack of alignment of beliefs about what should be done and how to enact it. Ideas and innovations are not in evidence, due to a highly unsafe learning environment for people to take risks, experiment or even give their opinions. The 'speaker for the opposition' seems to be the one who is heard the most, actively sabotaging any forward momentum that anyone is trying to achieve. The end result is that good people leave and you are left with the ones who should leave!

Neuroscience tells us that the corrosive environment is one in which most people are constantly in a state of threat. David Rock, author of *Your Brain at Work*, draws from a huge body of research to explain that the brain's limbic system has two organising principles: to minimise danger and maximise reward. When we are constantly 'on' and unconsciously alert for danger – 'I need to be wary or I will be attacked' – then withdrawal, attack or shut down are far more likely.

As a leader in an environment where these behaviours are being displayed, we need to walk and talk with courage, conviction and kindness – remembering that people are in fear so we need to create an environment of safety and accountability. Encourage positive professional behaviours and challenge those people keeping you at the corrosive level. Behaviours ignored are behaviours condoned. Are there behaviours you are accepting that you shouldn't be? Is there clarity about what you do expect?

The key action to move from this stage is: *lead with courage and kindness.*

2. Complacency

Complacency is the danger zone for any organisation. It creates a culture of 'near enough is good enough' where everyone is comfortably doing what they have always done.

The complacency zone has a lot of what I call *leaners*. These people do a whole lot of ... the bare minimum. The behaviour can be really hard to call because it just scrapes through as acceptable. It certainly doesn't create an environment of growth and momentum. I liken it to people who spend a lot of time leaning on the fence of comfort.

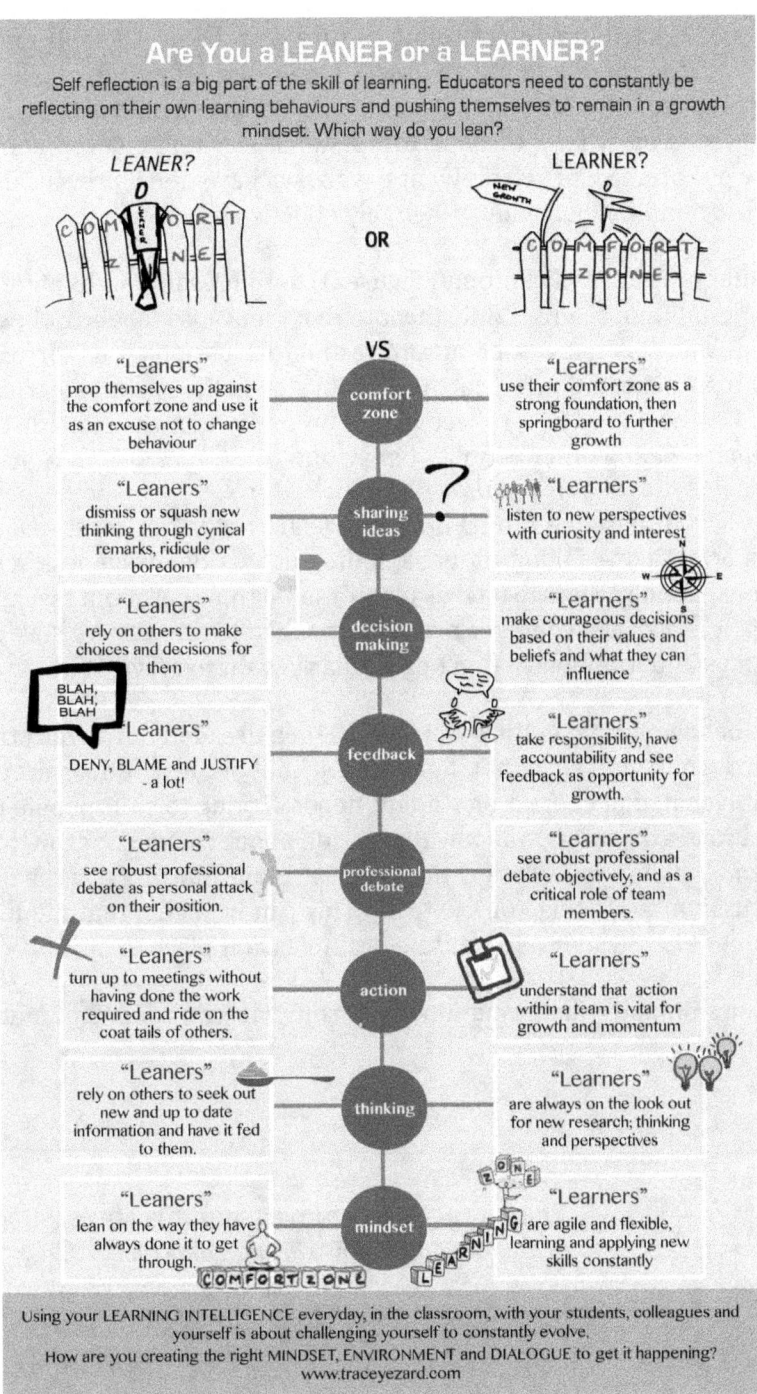

Figure 3 – Leaner or Learner Dichotomy

This type of behaviour and prevailing culture is probably the topic principals and school leaders talk about the most when discussing the challenges of leading change. The expected behaviours are not articulated and there is not a strong focus on what a thriving professional learning environment looks like. The old premise of 'we do what we always have done' prevails over the research around the behaviours in highly effective schools.

The Leaner or Learner dichotomy (Figure 3) outlines some areas of reflection for individuals and teams. While dichotomies can cause labeling of people if not used well, this list can be an interesting discussion focus for teams to identify their expectations. It can help them stay in the space of learning and growth. It is best used as a reflective tool on self within the team discussion rather than labeling other people's behaviour.

The *leaner* is a space we can be in when we are not in our most resourceful place as a learner – falling on behaviours such as defensiveness, avoiding work or expecting others to feed us inspirational thinking about teaching and learning. It is a space where we are very attached to the way we have always done things and from which don't particularly want to move.

Leaning behaviour and culture can lead us on a dreaded downward trend in the effectiveness and sustainability of the school because it doesn't respond to an ever-changing context or student needs. Trying to shift people to new behaviours is exhausting, and any discussion about change or growth is met with denial, blame and justification, or just plain quitting – be it quitting the discussion, the change or the team. This can be a sign that the learning environment is still seen as an unsafe or unpleasant place to be.

Do we see shift and transformation in the complacency zone? Not much.

The key action to move from this stage is:
articulate and follow through on expectations.

3. Confusion

A school in the confusion zone is constantly twirling around chasing its tail, knowing that *something* has to be done to address major issues and doing a whole lot of *stuff*, but not moving forward.

Schools use a large amount of data to track student improvement and the 'temperature' of the culture. Achievement data, assessment and feedback (both formal and informal) and student, staff and parent opinion surveys provide us with a clearer view of the relative success of our schools. Too often, though, the indicators are not responded to clearly enough.

In some schools the data is not used as part of the evaluation process, and certainly not as a tool to continually inform teaching. In these schools reflection that allows staff to analyse the impact of their teaching practice on student learning is either not an embedded practice or is not completed with any rigour. The crucial approach that *all teachers take responsibility for student learning* is still not part of the fabric of the school.

In the confusion zone there is a sense in the school that something needs to happen – but who knows what? There is a lack of outward focus – other schools or teachers who have had shifts in student learning are not examined or used as exemplars. Listening to or reading the educational experts is not an embedded learning practice. At this stage there is a genuine realisation that the school needs to change, but without clear leadership and collaboration on proactive approaches, the school can bounce from one 'silver bullet' to another, working reactively trying to find the magic elixir to its problems. The outcomes of the confusion zone are frustration and a feeling of being overwhelmed.

The key action to move from this stage is:
step back, take stock and create a plan.

4. Controversy

At this stage there is a clear understanding of the outcomes that need to be achieved, but people's hobbyhorses obstruct alignment to the best course of action.

If you have been in the corrosion zone, remnants of corrosive behaviour can bubble to the surface, with the more dominant voices getting traction on a particular direction while others don't feel aligned or even included in the solution. This level can echo some of the elements of the corrosive environment. The difference is that there is more goodwill in evidence. Celebration is warranted for getting to this stage, as it often reflects passion for getting better.

The key to keep moving up the ladder towards the buzz is to bring everyone into alignment over the direction you need to go in. It's important to involve your staff in robust discussion about the current context: achievement data, school culture, quality of teaching and learning and, of course, the level of collaboration and learning within the professional learning community. This is also a perfect time to revisit and realign the vision for the school and the values on which it stands. When establishing the vision for the school, the leadership team and staff need to discuss (and thrash out) the differences of opinion on the direction and the approach.

As a leader, you have to confidently lead these divergent conversations so that you are *all* having the robust discussion, rather than only a few dominant voices driving the agenda. Be careful not to leap onto every shiny new thing, take time to pause and clarify *where* you need to go and then how.

If you and your team are not aligned and the team is going in all directions, too much energy is placed into putting out fires, posturing and jumping for those new shiny things to solve problems. Not only that – your staff are still left in the confusion zone as they watch the people with influence directing them forward to different paths.

The key action to move from this stage is: *facilitate discussions that allow divergence and positive debate, then move to alignment.*

5. Clarity

The clarity zone indicates great promise for the school. People are clear on direction and the need for any initiatives or changes.

There is a team of committed individuals and pockets of teams collaborating and creating an environment of learning from each other. Teams challenge each other to reach their potential. It may be that the leadership team is very clear on what needs to be done and the rest of the staff are happy to be led. Momentum picks up as people see the way forward. The environment is one of optimism and energy. The conversations are more than likely to be about the work and the behaviours, more about learning to work differently.

The key action to move from this zone is: *co-create the vision and strategy with your whole team.*

6. Committed Collaboration – The Buzz

When this stage is reached, the energy of the learning within the team and the school fuels the momentum.

Teams are focused on working together, learning from each other, implementing and trialing different approaches. Leadership no longer has to create the change; the change and the desire to transform come from within. There is a positive buzz in the workplace – one that staff and students can feel. Leaders need to be skilled at growing potential and empowering staff to contribute and collaborate. Places that achieve this stage attract and grow great people.

There is also a high level of internal accountability in this zone. A *leaner* is not welcome in this environment – staff members understand that leaning behaviour brings down their effectiveness and ability to have strong, accountable and exciting conversations about where they are going and how they are getting there.

In this zone the majority of teachers – and other people working in the school – are passionate about students and student learning. Not only that, most are incredibly hard workers. They deserve to be trusted and to be part of the solution to the challenges of creating a rich, engaging and successful school, as well as crafting the vision of where the school is heading.

It is hard work, but it's rewarding and crucial to create a school that can respond to the rapid increase of complexity in the world they are trying to arm students to deal with.

Richard DuFour, in his essay 'Learning by Doing' also sees this hard work as essential if we are to truly make a difference within our schools:

The professional learning community concept does not offer a short cut to school improvement. It presents neither a program nor a recipe. It does provide a powerful, proven conceptual framework for transforming schools at all levels, but alas, even the grandest design eventually degenerates into hard work. A school staff must focus on learning rather than teaching, work collaboratively on matters related to learning, and hold itself accountable for the kind of results that fuel continual improvement. When educators do the hard work necessary to implement these principles, their collective ability to help all students learn inevitably will rise. If they fail to demonstrate the discipline to initiate and sustain this work, their school is unlikely to become more effective, even if those within the school claim to be a professional learning community. The rise or fall of the professional learning community concept in any school will depend not on the merits of the concept itself, but on the most important element in the improvement of any school—the collective capacity, commitment, and persistence of the educators within it.

When a school has reached the pinnacle of the ladder of the Six Stages of the Buzz, the other vitally important groups – students and families – are well and truly partners in the collaborative culture evident in the school. Of course committed collaboration doesn't happen overnight, even once this level has been reached. It is developed while you develop your staff. (Maintaining this stage is the subject of another book altogether!) Needless to say, student engagement, community engagement, the whole school–home partnership is a crucial part of a thriving school learning environment.

The key action to stay in this stage is: *constantly provide opportunities for your high-performance team is to co-create and innovate.*

3. GROWTH MINDSET

BELIEFS AND ASSUMPTIONS

At the base of our mindset sits our beliefs. Very often we don't even know what our beliefs are, as we have never really had to articulate them.

Beliefs drive our attitudes, behaviours and decisions, so having a clear idea of what we actually do believe is pretty important. I also think that many of our beliefs are really quite flexible – they can be shaped, changed, deepened, even made completely irrelevant. When I was five years old I believed that Shane Gibson in my prep class was the guy I was going to marry. He left the school when we were in Year 2 and my belief changed in the blink of an eye!

John Hattie, one of the world's global thought leaders in learning – both for students and teachers – says that the theories teachers hold (their beliefs) are incredibly strong and that if we don't try to understand what they are, where they come from and what they are based on, we are 'walking the hill all the way' in trying to gain traction.

Beliefs come from our personal 'map of the world', in other words the unique way we see the world. Often as leaders we can set about bringing on change in schools through simply trying to change behaviours and systems rather than addressing the underlying beliefs. If beliefs drive behaviour then this is where we need to focus our energies first so that the behaviours follow. One of the most effective ways of exploring our beliefs is by understanding why we do things. Unpacking the 'why' allows us to explore the basis of our assumptions, and add new perspectives and information to those beliefs. And perhaps change them.

Think back a number of years and pick a particular area that you had as a whole-school focus that is now done very differently. For example how you assessed student achievement, or student welfare, or how you planned your curriculum. What was the original approach? Were student engagement, wellbeing and curriculum seen as separate, unrelated things?

Exploring Beliefs

1. What did we do?

2. Why did we do it that way?

Because we needed to ...

It was known to ...

It encouraged ...

We assumed ...

Assessment showed ...

3. Beneath the why, what beliefs were driving all of the above?

4. How you do it now? What beliefs drive the way you currently do it?

If you do things quite differently now, you'll see that the beliefs may be quite different. They have probably been informed by evidence-based research, learning from experts, your own learning and evaluation, or by the evolving context of your school.

To achieve real change we need to explore our beliefs deeply. Much of the leadership and change-management literature ensures we start with why. Sometimes staff need help to understand the why thoroughly. It's not always as obvious as we think and yet understanding promotes certainty and commitment.

Using experts to help you shape beliefs is the place to start when it comes to building a strong *why* for people. Opening people's eyes to the evidence and best practice around the world can help them test their current beliefs. It can be a 'conscious convincer' that a change is needed – even if slightly – and can start to help them understand the more practical applications that need to follow. Simon Sinek's Ted Talk on *Start With Why* is a great resource for understanding *why* we should start with why, as are his books.

Here is an example of a belief that may drive the way you and your staff work as educators:

> *If teachers are to change, they need to participate in a professional learning community that is focused on becoming responsive to students ... As an intervention on its own, a collegial community will often end up merely entrenching existing practice and the assumptions on which it is based.*
>
> John Hattie & Helen Timperley, 'The Power of Feedback',
> *Review of Educational Research*

This is a pretty clear belief: teaching should be focused on responding to students. No matter the intervention (the what and the how), the belief should be the driver for everything that follows: suitability, design, implementation, teaching practice, learning practice and evaluation.

In the past a completely different sets of beliefs drove teaching. Students were left to struggle through concepts they didn't understand when the teacher taught it to them in the same way they had taught it for the last 10 years, regardless of who was in the class. A number of students either fell further behind or were bored because their education was either too easy or too hard. It was not *responsive*.

Have you had many *belief* conversations with your staff? These conversations help us understand each other more and move to a common set of underpinning principles to drive behaviours. Belief conversations help build a compelling environment for staff learning, unearth assumptions and create authentic dialogue.

Exploring Professional Learning Communities' Beliefs

Let's take this thinking about beliefs and apply it to the 'why' of professional learning communities.

1. Before you read any further, write down some of your beliefs about professional learning communities. Why should we focus on them? What values should underpin them? How should we think about them? Complete this activity before going on to part 2.

2. On page 119 I share some of my beliefs. As you read them, think about whether they resonate with you or not. Do you get a distinct 'agree' in your mind, a distinct 'don't agree' or a neutral response?

3. Which beliefs on either your list or my list drive the way you behave as a leader of your learning community? What would you add? How would others describe your beliefs?

Beliefs are fundamental to our sense of being. I often ask groups to ponder these two questions around beliefs:

Are your beliefs helping you get where you want to go?

Is each one helping you live your purpose?

Beliefs Can Shift in a Moment

Beliefs are unconscious drivers that really can be very shaky – yet we can hold onto them like they are made of iron and concreted into the ground.

The school my children attend has a consultant, Julie, working with the staff every now and again. She drives a lovely car and it is often seen parked right outside the school in the parking spot designated for people with a disability. Julie happens to be a friend and colleague of mine. One day a school mum said to me, 'She really should not be parking in the disabled parking – it's not a good look'. The school mum believed Julie was using the car park without any right to. 'Ah,' I said, 'that would probably be because she only has one leg'.

Did the school mum's belief change in the blink of an eye? Absolutely! She had just received a bit more data to help her shape a new belief.

If we open ourselves up to our beliefs being movable, our ability to have flexible and adaptable responses increases.

FIXED versus GROWTH MINDSET

A fixed mindset is one where our beliefs are set in proverbial concrete – hard to move and impossible to penetrate. A fixed mindset can also be less obvious and quite unintentional. In her book *Mindset: How You Can Fulfil Your Potential* Professor Carol Dweck talks about the power of our mindset and the effect a growth mindset can have on our ability to fulfill our potential, compared to a fixed mindset.

It is a highly relevant book for educators and reminds us of the importance of students understanding that if they believe they can improve – no matter the stage they're at – and that mistakes are an integral part of learning, their potential can be realised. We must also apply this to ourselves.

Dweck's perspective is that people with fixed mindsets see intelligence as static. If we are stuck in a fixed mindset we have a strong need to look smart. When we need to look smart we feel threatened by the success of others, rather than being inspired by them. This is one of the most ignored characteristics of growth and learning.

Actually, we need to be observing those who are doing great things and emulating them, pinching ideas from them, integrating their approach into the way we work.

In other words, we should model their excellence and apply it in our context.

When was the last time you looked at someone doing great things in an area in which you needed to develop skills or achieve? Instead of watching them, or talking to them and taking note on how they were doing it, did a bit of 'I'll never be able to do that' (denial) or ' I'd be able to do that if I had the time to focus on it' (justification) or 'I can't do that because my family/work/dog/guinea pig situation doesn't let me' (blame) come up for you?

The Comparison Crisis

One of the most crippling mindset blocks is the one of comparison. Instead of curiosity and a desire to grow, the thinking is one that sends us into envy, jealousy and futility. This needs to be moved out of the way before we can learn by watching others who we believe are achieving 'better' than us.

Neuroscience tells us that if we see each other as competitors we code each other as foes. I find that juicy! It's great to gain insight into how our brain really is running the show. So watch our for that stab of jealousy, envy or moroseness, identified by 'I'll never be as good as …' or 'they're going to take my job if I'm not careful.' Stop! Give yourself a metaphoric slap on the face and get on with finding out as much as you can about what they do and how they do it. Start *learning* from them.

When writing *The Buzz* I copped my own metaphoric slap. I was stuck in a fixed mindset – 'I can't do this; I'm not a writer' and 'look at Sue – she's written four books. How does she do it!?' To counter it I told my two children I was going to write a certain number of words before the morning. I acknowledged the fixed mindset that was keeping me from growing and then reframed my thinking. I drew on some of the approaches that have worked for writerly colleagues of mine. I used the term 'bum glue' to help focus on what needed to be done, put 'WRITE THE BOOK' on my screen saver and created an accountability tally with a colleague who was good enough to hassle me.

When we get over ourselves and realise that if we take action we can learn from others, we learn so much. All over the world amazing shifts are occurring for students because of incredibly gifted and generous teachers. We need to tap into them and observe them with a learning eye.

Think of all the less-than-useful mindset thoughts that can get in our way:

What if I fail?

What if I look stupid?

What if the class plays up?

What if they do it better than I do?

How will I feel if I don't do it right?

I studied this for years; I don't need to change the way I work.

I've never been any good at this.

I don't want to play.

I already do this perfectly well.

On and on and on … How depressing, not to mention draining on the energy.

What about if we thought instead:

What if I give it a go?

What's the worst thing that can happen?

I am sure going to learn something – not sure what but that doesn't matter.

What if I tried to fail?

This will be fun!

Let's see what happens.

Even a master was once a beginner.

Small steps.

I feel energised, motivated and ready to dive in!

Time to refresh.

It will only add to my understanding.

We ask students take these approaches all the time.

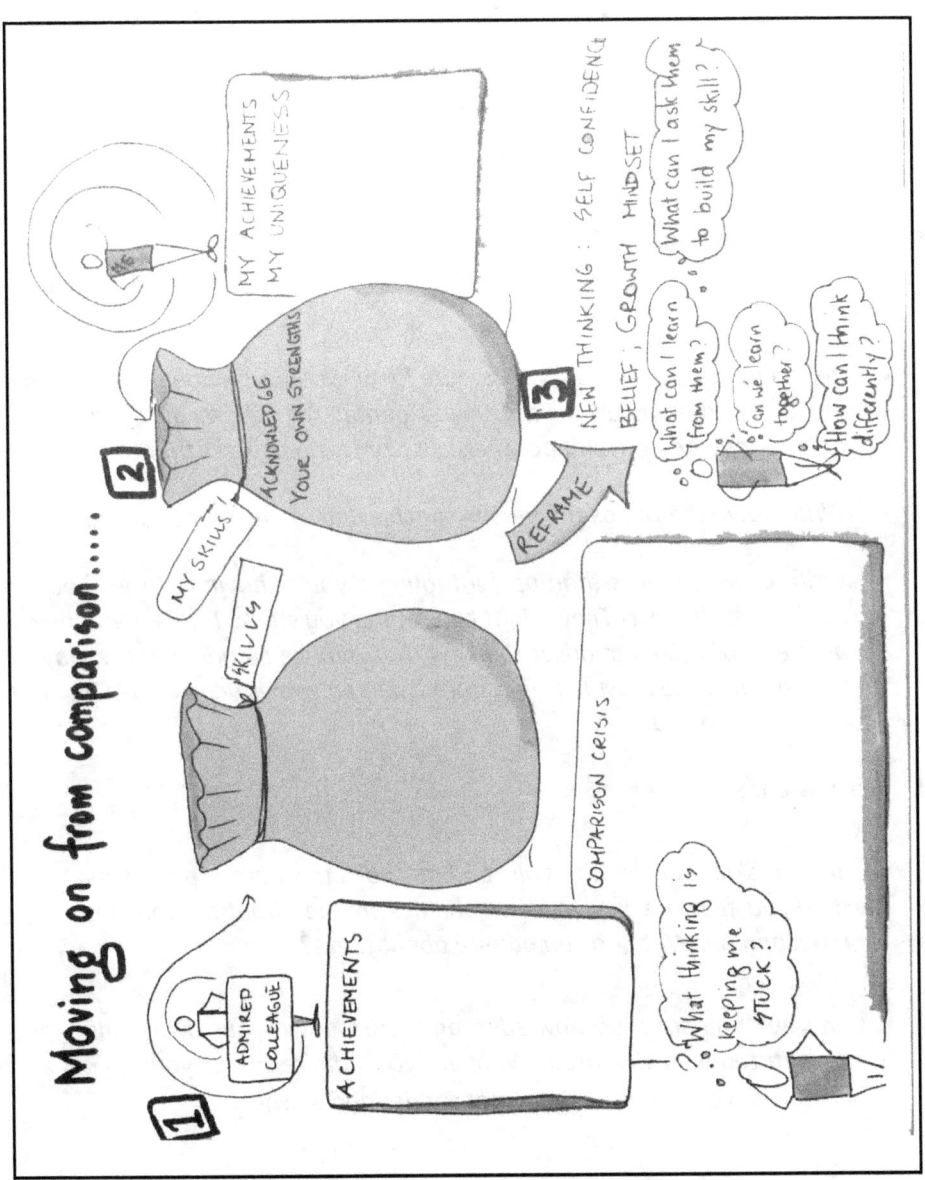

Figure 4 – Comparison Crisis Worksheet

Reflect On The Comparison Crisis

1. Identify

    - Reflect on a person whom you admire for what they are doing, but you can identify a 'comparison crisis'. Can you identify small elements of 'jealousy' or 'poor me' or 'I haven't got the skills/context resources that they have'?

    - Write down the things the person is achieving in the left hand box.

    - Write down the less-than-useful thoughts you're having in the thought bubble – be honest! They might be keeping you stuck. This is about being aware of any fixed mindset thinking that may be standing in the way of your gaining the most learning from a person who is achieving in an area of interest to you.

2. Acknowledge

    - In **their** skill sack, list the skills and attitudes this person possesses that you feel are key to their abilities in the situation you are reflecting on. What do you admire about them?

    - In **your** skill sack, acknowledge and write down your own skills and attitudes in this area. What do you admire about yourself? Celebrate yourself as an educator, leader and learner.

3. Reframe

    - Reframe the thoughts you were having about the person into thoughts that acknowledge their strengths and any growth mindset beliefs that would be useful for you to focus on. (Consider: What will I try? How can I support myself to try this? What small step will I attempt first?)

4. Focus

- Bringing these two skill sacks together, set out a plan that helps you to see that person as a role model – what can you learn from observing this person? Can you talk to them about their approach, their beliefs and the way they have gone about their process? Which of these can you test, apply and use in your own skill development? Which skills of your own will you build on to stretch your growth?

Don't Be A Victim Of Your Specialty

Dr Briony Scott, Principal of Wenona School in North Sydney, is a great advocate of the growth-mindset approach and talks to educators about the need to make sure specialisation, or expertise, doesn't cause us to tighten control around our mindset and create a fixed state. A fixed state means we are not open to others' ideas and thoughts, new thinking and approaches. The more we think we know about something, the more we need to consciously let go of control to free our growth mindset to be expansive rather than restrictive.

The Comfort Zone/Learning Zone Paradigm

The term 'comfort zone' tends to get thrown around a lot but I think it's useful to understand that stepping outside of our comfort zones means we are in our *learning zones*. This stretch enables growth. When I ask people to identify what they feel outside their comfort zone, the most prevalent answers from staff without a thriving learning culture are:

- Anxiety
- Stress
- Anger
- Frustration
- Fear
- Increased heart rate, perspiration, butterflies.

In fact it is very possible to be out of your comfort zone, in the learning zone, and have the following feelings:

- Excitement
- Anticipation
- Motivation
- Enthusiasm
- Clarity
- Increased heart rate, perspiration, butterflies.

Far more compelling! These are the feelings we want to access when using our learning intelligence. They help us create a compelling environment.

The DBJs (The Deny, Blame, Justify Game)

Sometimes at an unconscious level we can be so attached to our comfort zone that we decide we are not going to play in the learning zone at all. I first learnt this paradigm through my Neuro-Linguistics Programming (NLP) training many years ago. It was a real eye opener for me and a great tool to identify the excuses I used to stay in my comfort zone. I tend to use this model with people keen to step outside their comfort zones as individuals and groups – people who want to understand how to create the mindset, environment and dialogue, and get better results.

In our minds and out of our mouths come all the reasons to stay comfortable – all the denial, blame, justifications and sometimes plain 'I quit'. You may have heard a few of these before:

I haven't got time.

The way we used to do it was fine.

The instructions have not been clear enough.

We did this in 1994, and 2004, and now again ...

I'm not trained to do that.

It's not my yard duty; see the teacher on duty.

I've already shown you how to do this – why aren't you understanding it?

There is no way I am going to do that!

The excuses come almost by default if we are feeling anywhere near a reactive state of mind. It's a reaction to not wanting to be out of the comfort zone and can happen at an unconscious level. We can be simply unaware it is happening. Yet brain research is identifying the need for us to get out of our comfortable ways of doing things for our brain's sake. Agility and flexibility are the exercise our brains need to keep in top condition.

Are You a Ninja?

By now you may have identified a few 'DBJers' on your staff. People who, when asked to do or think differently, speak a fountain of DBJs.

Congratulations. You have mastered Brown Belt!

Brown Belt

Many people go through life never understanding that excuses are a way to keep comfortable. Even being able to identify them in others is a huge skill. Brown Belt masters can identify phrases in others that are comfort-zone strategies. They recognise a threat situation and understand that the person is putting up all the reasons for not wanting to leave their comfort zone.

Black Belt

The next level is much harder – identifying excuses in ourselves. Not only are we able to identify them when they come out of our mouths, we can also identify them when they are swimming around in our heads. Watching and listening to our thoughts is a skill that comes from being close to a 'meta' position in our thinking. It's De Bono's blue hat working in the brain[1]. We often spend our lives not controlling much of the chatter that goes on in our heads and forget how powerful these little sentences can be. But, depending on their quality, they change our mindset, emotions and behaviours. It's where we get sayings such as: 'Glass half empty or half full' and Henry Ford's 'Whether you think you can or you can't, you're right'.

While there are many factors that can create failing schools or toxic environments, I have seen a strong connection between this context and DBJ language that comes out of the leadership team's mouth. Cleaning up our internal and external talk can make a huge difference to how we see the world. In turn, this shift helps us work with more optimism and see opportunities, rather than blame the world for the problems in our own yard.

Ninja

The Ninja level is the level of the artful leader. They can spot DBJs in others, and hear it internally and externally in themselves – just like a Black Belt. And they have one more defining quality: they can reframe others and pull themselves from a DBJ mindset into a proactive one. They  help create a thriving environment of learning for themselves and others. This involves building safety nets for people in the learning zone. Ninjas have great learning intelligence.

The opposite of DBJ is the ARAE — the Acceptance, Responsibility, Accountability and Engagement mindset. In this mindset we know that we ultimately have a degree of influence and control over what happens and how we respond. This mindset is the one stimulates growth and ensures a proactive, action-oriented approach. This is not the 'Isn't life dreamy?' view of the world, it's the pragmatic approach: 'What needs to be done? Let's do it.'

---

1. Edward DeBono's Six Thinking Hats are used in both business and educational contexts to strengthen our ability to solve problems by accessing six different thinking strategies.

The blind spots of our unconscious competence

We all have skills and behaviours that are our strengths, our unconscious competencies. We are so comfortable with them that we no longer have to focus on them, as they come so naturally to us.

To improve self-reflection and self-awareness of the comfort zone, try to identify the areas of your unconscious competence that are currently not serving you well. This can be a stretch, as some of the stuff we are so good at we don't even recognise. They are in a blind spot of our thinking. You might be incredibly skilled at procrastination or a master of making things harder than they are. Or maybe you are an exemplary self-doubter!

Instead can you shine a light on and get serious about becoming *incompetent*? Sometimes we need to unravel the comfort zone to really check where our blind spots might be and establish some game-changers. I am highly skilled, for example, at putting other things ahead of the most important yet difficult thing I have to do. Amazing how important replying to that email or finding that particular website is when a deadline is coming up. The habitual ways we have of working, thinking or interacting with others are perfect examples of our comfort zone at work and, put simply, some of it works for us and some of it doesn't. Our challenge is to get serious about developing incompetence in these areas!

Safety-net strategies

Feeling comfortable out of our comfort zone sounds like an oxymoron. But it is through putting in place thinking, activities and processes that support us in the learning zone that we can feel safer to be there.

There will always be people who are challenged by change and stepping outside the comfort zone. So the safety nets they put in place are vital ways to help them maintain a thriving learning zone. Every person in the learning community must take responsibility for their learning-zone safety net. The leadership team alone can't provide it.

Every person should understand how they learn best, how to support their own needs and how to access these supports. This is as much about self-awareness and self-regulation as anything else. If we leave it up to others to provide, we are staying on the DBJ side of life ('I never get enough PD', 'No one gave me time to practise', 'I didn't understand the requirements').

Stephen Covey, the guru of *7 Habits of Highly Effective People*, talks about stepping out of our 'circle of concern' into our 'circle of influence'. His model is to take action and do something that helps us take responsibility, rather than being the victim. This mindset is again about movement and action, sitting in a place of 'doing' rather than in a reactive space where things are being 'done to'.

CASE STUDY

Bushey Academy is a school in the United Kingdom that was under what is referred to as Special Measures, where the school inspection agency deemed it to be failing in its ability to provide quality education, and lacking the leadership to create improvement. With a new leadership team and a strong plan, they moved from this Special Measures label to being the third most improved school in the country. The Head, Andrew Hemmings, cites one of the major reasons as being the shift in focus of the educators' mindset from one of behaviours to one of progress, and that this change in thinking led to professional behaviours that drove improvement.

> We have a relentless focus on progress. We've got a 'vulnerable groups' crew that meet every four weeks. They talk about all the different vulnerable groups and students and how we can narrow the gap there. We can get the students there. That's our new mindset.
>
> We also focus on teaching. We've got some great teachers here and we share good practice. A real openness and transparency and a willingness to share and learn from each other, that's been really important.
>
> Andrew Hemmings, 'Talking Heads: How We Pulled our School out of Special Measures' *The Guardian*

Team Activity: Comfort Zone/Learning Zone

1. Identify

    - *As a team, reflect on feelings that keep us in our comfort zone. What makes the comfort zone attractive?*

    - *Now move to the space outside the comfort zone. Consider the feelings/reactions that come up for us outside the comfort zone. Is there a difference between when we choose to get out of our comfort and when it is thrust upon us? Discuss experiences when you've had little choice, and your attitude and mindset have allowed you stay in the learning zone in a resourceful and thriving way. Discuss times when you have consciously decided to step out and try something new.*

2. Strategies

    - *Together, identify the safety net strategies that work for you all as individuals and as a team so that the learning zone is a positive place to be. Look at how you can strengthen them and make them work for you as learners.*

3. Plan

    - *Put in place a plan to implement and evaluate your strategies.*

HIGH CHALLENGE HIGH SUPPORT

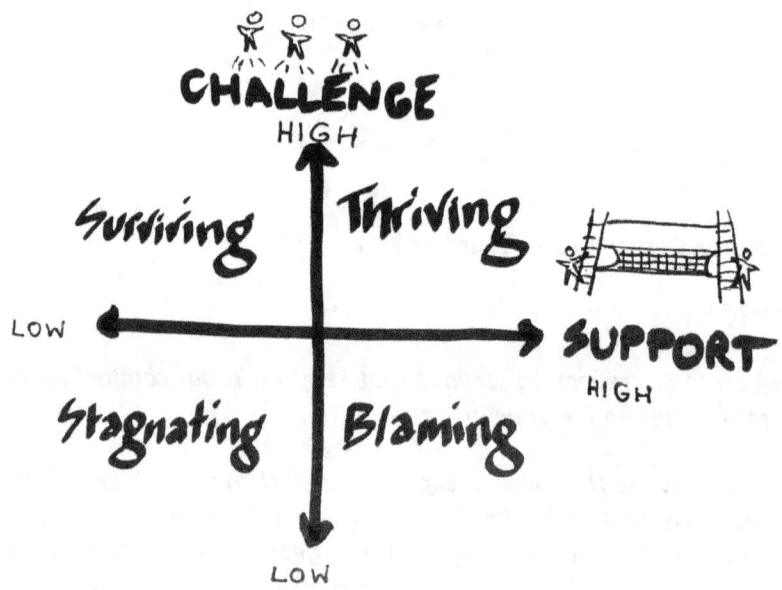

Figure 5 – High Challenge High Support

High Challenge

A fundamental element of a strong, *buzzy* learning environment for educators is a high-challenge mindset. It's not enough to have a good team environment where people are exposed to great professional learning, without clear expectations that the learning is trialed, tested and evaluated. There needs to be a focus on results that are about progress, learning and responsive teaching. I have seen great teams come to a shuddering halt during self-evaluations because they haven't focused enough on progress and growth in student learning, just like the situation Andrew Hemmings found at Bushey Academy.

We need to inspire and challenge ourselves to push potential. Keep on setting an environment that is always about the students and giving them the best possible milieu for learning and growing. To be perfectly frank, sometimes I think principals are so reticent to put more pressure on their staff that the thing that suffers the most is growth. Consider the following:

It's okay – everyone is working their backsides off; we're doing pretty well.

We're doing as well as we can with our demographic and the state of the school resources.'

We've got a good team – I don't want to pressure them.

If you identify with this, then get smart about making the key elements of *The Buzz* work for you. Collaborate with your staff to identify the challenges and strategies to deal with them. During these conversations, focus the team on their strengths and areas of achievement and a high-challenge/high-support mindset will become part of the fabric of how your team works, rather than an add-on.

High Support

With high challenge must come high support. Educational leaders need to care about teachers so that the teachers feel they have a secure and safe foundation and are trusted. Innovation and creativity are more likely from a position of safety. Empathy, compassion, strong connections and support from leaders are core to a high-challenge environment. Some of the educational leaders I admire most are able to show empathy and understanding to those teachers who have given them the most grief over the years. They acknowledge the strengths these teachers bring to the school and the growth they have made. They genuinely care about them and see them as an individual with aspirations, concerns and history.

Support needs to be twofold – internal and external. This means individuals internally supporting themselves through their mindset and their actions while the safety nets provided by the team and school add to this. We want to make sure we are a group of proactive learners, not victims who need spoon-feeding to make any sort of leap. We need to be educators with a strong internal locus of control. We need to drive ourselves and be immersed in an environment that supports independent adult learners.

Which Quadrant are we in?

1. Reflect

   Look at Figure 5 then reflect on your team and its challenge and support environment. Where does it sit? Which quadrant are you in with your safety-net strategies and your expectations of results?

2. Question

   Have you created high support, but perhaps not high challenge, and so are experiencing 'expectant' or 'blaming' behaviours? Are your staff looking to you and the leadership team to provide everything needed for new knowledge, without any expectation on your part to have them implement it? I call this the Princess Syndrome.

   Perhaps you have a high-challenge environment and your staff are operating in a survival mindset because there is not enough support.

   Or is there low support and low challenge? Is the focus on the professional learning environment a low priority, have people have been stagnating (in the complacency zone)?

3. Sit on the Balcony

   While this self-reflection and balcony consideration of what is happening within your school may be difficult, thankfully there are many things you can do to build the learning intelligence and create that thriving learning culture you are after.

CURIOSITY

A curious mind is endlessly searching for different interpretations of the world.

The world would be a much better place if we were more curious and less judging. Being curious helps our minds to be active, rather than passive, growing, rather than fixed. Curiosity comes from a position of not knowing it all and from wanting to find out more. It also helps us to be more open-minded. When we are curious, we are open to information and ideas that could change our perceptions, beliefs and approaches to life. There is an excitement in the curious mind! You never know what might come next or which adventure is just around the corner. There is a sense of wonder present in the minds of the curious.

Does this mean you need to be an intrepid explorer to be truly curious? I really don't mean it to be that extreme. One of my good friends and colleagues has a continuously curious mind. Sitting with a coffee chatting about a whole range of things, I am always amazed by the interesting questions he asks me to find out what I really think about things. Quite often I have to take a long pause to reflect on just what I do think about the question he asked, as I hadn't been curious enough to really delve in deep.

I have learnt much from his approach. The really interesting thing for me is that he never judges my answer. He is genuinely interested and curious about my view of the world. I try to model his excellence and ask questions of people just to find out their thoughts, perspectives and ideas – not to pass any judgment, or give any advice. To be able to do this well, an authentic interest in others and the world around is important.

Warning on the label

When it comes to being curious with others, don't confuse interest and curiosity with intrusiveness!

There is a fine line here. We need to use our emotional awareness of others to build rapport – active and genuine interest in them is a great way to do this – but we also need to make sure we are not crossing the line into 'creepy' territory. Usually I find education professionals with the curiosity mindset are skilled with this, as they generally have a strong emotional awareness of others. But if you know you tend to put people off by asking too many questions, you might need to rethink your approach.

A genuinely curious person is not judgemental. It's not about seeing yourself as right, because you actually don't have just one interpretation of the world.

There is a shop not far from my home that sells items made by local artisans. It is filled with amazing pieces that you can't find in the chain stores and shopping centres. Colleen, the passionate and committed woman who started the shop, is creating a real community hub where people drop by to chat, have a cup of coffee and share stories. People from all walks of life come to the store – artists, crafters, people experiencing homelessness, people just wanting to connect, others seeking great gifts to buy.

Many people tell Colleen the most amazing things. Because of the compelling environment she has created, and her own sense of curiosity about the world, people share insights that may otherwise have been overlooked.

One day a tiny woman in her eighties came into the shop while I was there. They began to chat and I learnt something new. There is an established folklore that when mothers and wives received letters from their men during the two World Wars, they would immediately put the kettle on. I had always assumed it was to have a nice cup of tea and be able to sit down to read the letter – the most obvious answer. But the there was a far more interesting reason. Many of the men would write where they were stationed under the stamp, and the women used the kettle to produce steam off the stamp so they could know where their loved ones were situated.

Colleen has conversations that head into interesting directions because she asks interesting questions. How many interesting facts, insights or opinions do your staff have that you don't know because you've never asked?

The key

Curiosity is the key mindset of a professional learning environment. What does it look like, sound like and feel like for you? What do we gain through curiosity? We gain a feeling of anticipation, a shift in position and an opportunity to wonder what else might be out there if we look through someone else's eyes. Simply asking your team what they are curious about when it comes to a major initiative or plan you have for the school can unearth some fascinating perceptions and views of the world – and increase a growth mindset.

Today the internet provides easy access to answers to virtually any question. When my daughter was about seven years old, she typed into Google 'Is Santa Claus real?' Fortunately for her, as she desperately wanted him to be, her just-emerging research skills were happy with the first website that came up, which gave the wise perspective that if you do believe in him, then he is real. This was good enough for her!

Increasing our Curiosity

1. Internal Curiosity

    Do something in a way you've always done it. It may be the way you set yourself up for the day's work, or how you interact with a certain person, or how you do a particular task. Now ask yourself some questions:

    Why do I do it that way?

    What are my beliefs and assumptions about that?

    What has led me to those beliefs and assumptions?

    Even though this may seem like a silly thing to do for a reasonably menial task, this step will make you more agile at diving down into your beliefs, which is something we need to be able to do to increase our learning intelligence. We know beliefs drive behaviours. They can also expose some flawed thinking or lack of thinking about the way you do something if your beliefs are outdated, uneducated or lacking in substance.

    Sometimes when we dig into why we do something we unearth some interesting understandings:

    Because that was how I was taught as a child and I believe it is the way it should be done.

    Because I am really familiar with it and I can do it on auto pilot, so I believe it is the easiest way.

    Because it is the way I have been doing it for years and it gets results.

(This is great if it doesn't have any negative consequences – think of a head chef who throws boiling pans at the first-year apprentice to get them washed, yelling 'hot!' as they sail down the kitchen. He does it because that was how he was treated when he was an apprentice and the dishes always get done!)

Because I can't do it any other way.

The book *Rework: Change the Way You Work Forever* by David Heinemeier Hansson and Jason Fried is a great example of thinking differently. It tests our thinking about the way we work and helps us become more curious about doing it another way. It comes from the business world but, as always, there is a huge amount to learn about working differently by looking outside our own backyard.

Other questions to keep you curious about yourself:

What is my purpose for doing this job?

What makes me come alive?

Where do I see myself heading?

What are my greatest challenges?

If I learnt the most useful thing today, what would it help me do?

2. External Curiosity

- *Question*

Have a conversation with someone where you ask some really great questions simply to be curious. You could let them know beforehand that you are trying an experiment with curiosity. I suggest you choose a mentor, peer or friend that you know quite well. Start a conversation about something in their lives. Ask them some questions relating to the situation, their actions or reflections.

- *Reflect*

What happened? What was important to them about it? What did they learn from it? What were they hoping to have come out of it?

Don't pass any judgment or give any possible solutions. Reflect afterwards by yourself, or perhaps with your conversation partner, about what you learnt or how you saw the world differently.

Be okay with uncertainty. There is a Zen saying: 'High understanding comes from not understanding at all.'

3. Team Curiosity

Curious questions for teams to help build a growth mindset:

What do we believe about how students learn?

What do we believe about how adults learn?

How do we identify quality teaching?

If we were to improve anything on our team, what would it be?

What are the things we should do more of? Less of?

What things have we implemented as a team that have made the biggest impact on students?

What would happen if we ... (did it on Tuesday, only drew pictures, started by asking another question, paused before answering, approached this differently)?

Could we get a different outcome doing something else?

How else could we do that?

How would (insert name/team) do that?

4. COMPELLING ENVIRONMENT

ARE YOU HOT?

Walking through the streets of the city on a warm Friday or Saturday night is a great way to check out which restaurants are 'hot' at the moment. Lines stretch down the pavement outside those that are hot and don't take bookings. Instead, you're greeted with, 'We'll take your number – you should be okay in about an hour.' Similarly, people with disappointed faces are turned away from those hot restaurants that do take bookings but have overflowing reservations already.

Whatever the secret ingredients are – and you can be pretty sure there is great food and probably great service as well – there is something compelling about the space that people are drawn to. Word of mouth probably had a lot to do with it and perhaps great reviews and an aura of hip, high quality and/or adventurousness. And it's not just new, shiny restaurants; discerning punters always return to the restaurants that give them what they are after. Some restaurants are difficult to get into no matter how long they've been in business.

Compelling environments create an atmosphere that people want to be a part of. To build the learning intelligence of our schools, we need to understand compelling learning environments for adults as well as students. What compels people to be in a learning state? What sort of place encourages to people want to work, achieve and improve together?

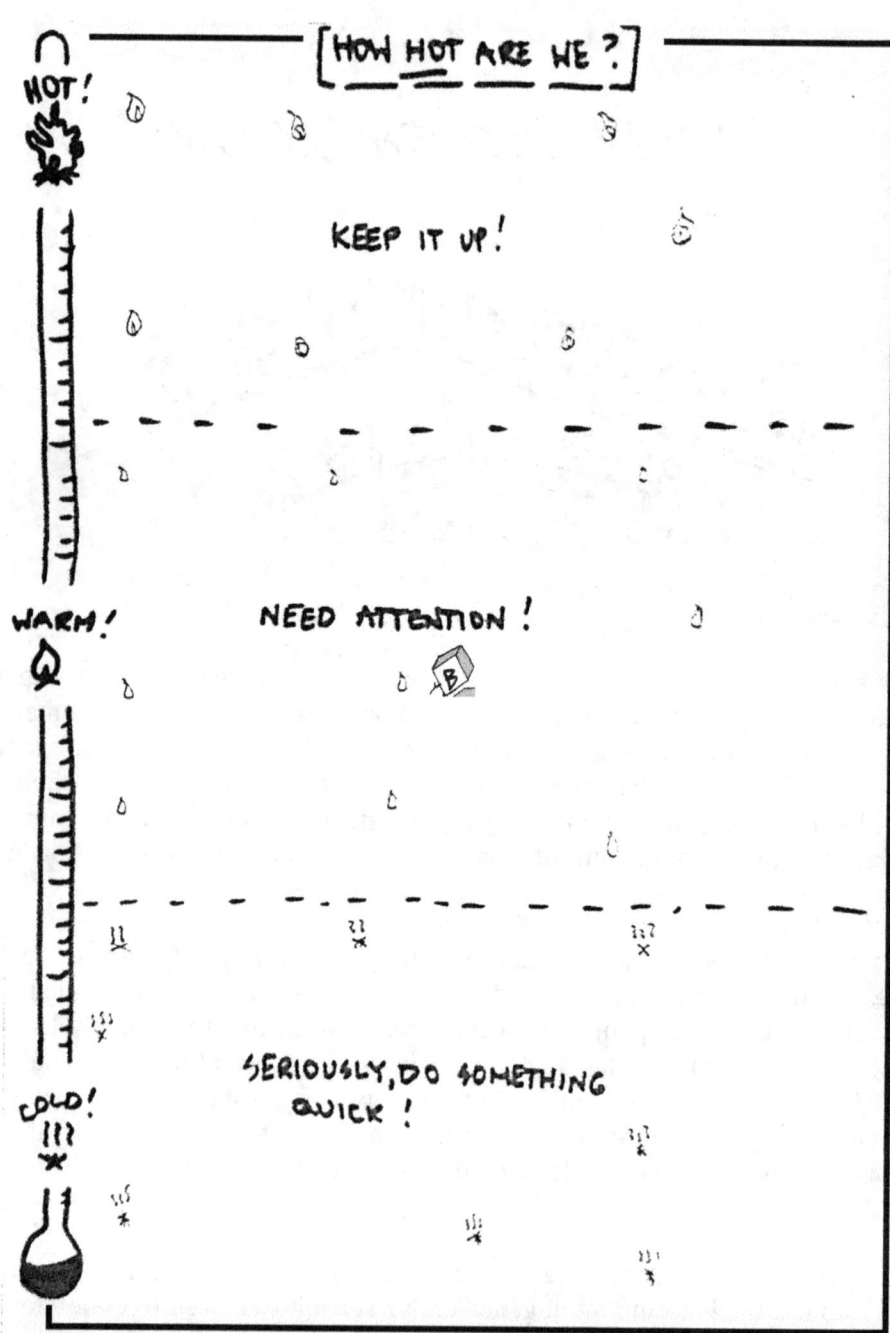

Figure 6 – Are You Hot?

Is your Environment Hot or Not?

Take a moment to pause and reflect. What components make a learning environment compelling from your perspective? List those areas that do have impact and other areas that actively destroy a thriving learning environment. What creates the buzz for you?

Figure 6 provides a template that can guide you as you reflect.

ENERGY

The energy in a school with a buzz is almost visible. When I ask people to articulate their understanding of this energy they talk about a sense of safety to be who they are (trust), an excitement about the work and a genuine enthusiasm to test their thinking and approaches to teaching and learning. There is also something about the way people with energy for team learning and collaboration hold their bodies, give eye contact, and in the quality of their tone.

I have seen the energy get completely sucked out of the people in a room by the entrance of their leader. People literally shift in their chairs and pull away from connecting with this person. The discussion falters to a monosyllabic interaction if the leader's energy is hostile and attacking. It swamps all hope of a thriving and compelling environment.

Sometimes you can feel this coming from one or two members of the group. They contribute generously to a corrosive environment! People do not want to share their opinions for fear of being 'shot down or shut down'. In this case the whole group needs to take control and create clear individual and team expectations and protocols. Taking this control requires courage and clear leadership from within. The most difficult situation for team members to deal with is when the leader is the problem.

Within a collegiate educator group everyone – either leader or member – has a professional responsibility to provide generative, collaborative energy that encourages contribution, not discourages it. Too often I find that a corrosive environment is a product of neglect and non-communication – distinctly non-compelling.

FUN AND POSITIVE INTENT

Another part of a high-energy, positive environment is that people have some fun and enjoy themselves!

I spent Christmas night last year in the Emergency Department with my husband's grandmother, who had broken both her wrists. As we waited for X-ray and CT-scan results to come back, I got the chance to observe the staff working in ED. Here it was, Christmas night, a full waiting room and beds full of people needing attention. And yet there was still a sense of humour around. One doctor had large Christmas bells in her ears. Not only could we hear her coming towards us, the bells also tinkled when she was on the other side of the department. Staff often had smiles on their faces and were making little jokes with patients to keep their spirits up.

Wherever I am I tend to be drawn to watching the staff interact with one another – call it an occupational habit. The large 'control' areas of an ED have people moving in and out rapidly, checking computers and charts, making calls. I noticed an easy goodwill and humour. They shared light-hearted banter and showed basic respect: eye contact, moving out of one another's way and speaking warmly even though the interaction may have been very quick.

Cris Popp, an innovation and laughter expert based in Melbourne, quotes Victor Borge when he encourages more laughter and humour in organisations: 'Laughter is the shortest distance between two people'. This resonates in a group context as well. Teams laughing and sharing an easy humour build strong rapport and trust with each other. Cris works with organisations to tap into this. His approach helps teams build trust.

Laughter is one of the most powerful team build/icebreakers because it involves a combination of positive affect and vulnerability. When we laugh, we are exposing ourselves, in a way that has a lot of positive hormones and other body chemicals associated with it. When we laugh in the presence of our colleagues and teammates, we are associating the state of feeling good, with that person – it is a powerful way to build trust.

Research into the impact of humour in leaders by the Hay Group in 2004 found a number of studies outlining the effects of positive humour on the workplace. It also cited research linking humour and emotional intelligence with transformational leadership. Humour that is sarcastic or uses put-downs dressed as jokes is not a great indicator of a safe, trusting environment. That's usually about a win/lose situation, with the joker doing all the winning.

While I am not suggesting that we should constantly be cracking jokes and playing pranks, we can come to our collaborative work and our collegiate interactions with a positive, light approach to what we are doing. Being able to make mistakes and learn from them requires a reasonable amount of levity, which says: 'Oh well, that went belly up – what do we do now?' Approaches that use humour and acceptance help us stay in a no-blame, action-oriented state.

In schools where the energy is not welcoming, fun or high in goodwill, some staff say, 'We don't have time for that stuff.' However, the staff in the Emergency Department didn't use that excuse.

A SAFE ENVIRONMENT

Significant research in neuroscience indicates that learning occurs far more effectively in an environment of perceived safety. Of course, this also has major implications for the classroom environment as well. In fact, nothing makes my blood boil more than seeing a teacher create a supposed 'learning environment' that is characterised by fear through belittling, ridiculing and patronising their students. Seriously – how can we expect students to learn to their potential if their brains are in fear mode? Arrggh! Teachers like that should *not* be teaching. The same can be said for leaders.

If we are in a threat or fear state then our brain forces us to withdraw, retreat, shutdown or become aggressive. Chemically our brains are flooded with adrenalin and cortisol, which fires our more primitive brain and sets off our survival instincts. By contrast, environments of safety create a reward state that increases the 'feel good' chemicals such as oxytocin and dopamine. Trust resides in a reward state, distrust in a threat state.

BUILDING SAFETY

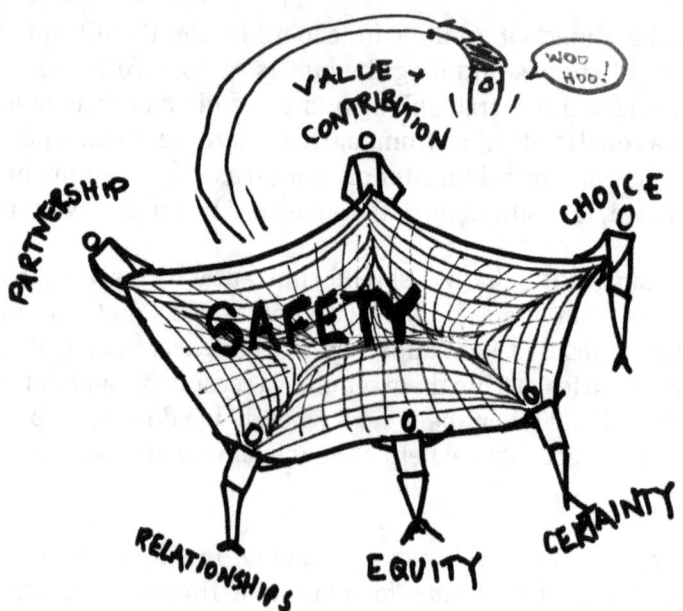

Partnership Not Hierarchy

People size up their place in a hierarchy very quickly. Think of those times when new people come into your school, either short term or long term. When the new person arrives, members of the group can make them feel safe in a couple of minutes by smiling and inviting them in, creating a partnership status through their dialogue. Alternatively, they can put them into a threat simply by looking them up and down and not interacting with them at all. This can be the domain of the 'clique': the 'in' group, which threatens others' safety by ensuring their own perceived position is higher through various unconscious ways.

Of course, if you're the new person one of the best approaches to any group is to not compare yourself to others. Be self-regulating and self-confident. If, on the other hand, you're part of a strong team, have a look around to see who might be on the periphery looking in. Invite them.

Choice

We all crave choice, from little choices to big choices. As humans we have an innate need to exert control over our environment. You may recognise people in your life for whom choice is very important. Take away their control or their choices and they step quickly into a threat response. A threat response can look like defensiveness, fear or withdrawal.

From a leadership perspective, when creating a learning environment for your staff, consider reflecting on those for whom choice is a big driver of safety. How could you increase their choice when introducing change or learning? Many schools embarking on peer observation have started out with every teacher identifying their learning needs, and their collaborators and mentors. This is a perfect example of giving control to the individual to help to create safety.

Patterns of Certainty

Our brains crave these moments of predictability and reliability. People like, for example, to understand the intentions of the meeting they're attending or have certainty around expectations of performance development plans. These help create certainty.

CASE STUDY

Over the last few years I have worked on leadership and strategy with organisations called Medicare Locals (MLs) within the health sector. These organisations were created to help integrate the health system to provide better access to community health services, take the pressure off acute hospitals and for various other goals.

In 2014, a review found a big variance in the success of these organisations. As a result the MLs were required to re-tender for their contracts under new specifications and objectives via new entities that covered greater catchments. Of course this caused huge anxiety in the staff, as it decreased the certainty of their employment. Many MLs suffered from low morale, gossip and staff members seeking jobs elsewhere. They were in a threat state and not coping as resourcefully as possible.

The ML I was working with had a strong internal culture of excellence, was values-driven and was doing great work with the community creating opportunities for better health outcomes. After the announcement about the possible end of the funding, the CEO ensured her staff were given updates weekly. She shared as much as she could. She and her executive were honest about their expectations for the future and were proactive about ensuring that ongoing program staff were in an environment that was true to their values of respect and integrity. They allowed their staff as much certainty as was possible within the confines of the context. As a result, they were able to keep many of their staff and these staff were better able to deal with the situation. When anyone did feel the need to move on, their endeavours to find a job were supported.

If you have managed closing or merging schools I am sure you will relate to the threat state that staff can go into as certainty decreases. Communication is the key to creating certainty. Even if you cannot create complete certainty, give them certainty about the process, the steps and the timeline, and *communicate*.

Friend or foe?

'Relatedness involves deciding whether others are "in" or "out" of a social group. Whether someone is friend, or foe.' David Rock.

The research shows that in the absence of safe social interaction people will code you as foe before any other label. This judgment occurs in the blink of an eye. It's unconscious. As a leader, if people are going to hear what I have to say, or be okay with me challenging their thinking or approach, I need to make sure they code me as friend as soon as possible. (It feels much better for all of us!) This is where we create trust, relationships and connection. Safe learning environments are built on these elements. It is the domain of a strong tribe – feeling accepted, included and valued.

Contribution and Value

One of the comments I hear from staff exhibiting threat behaviours is that their contribution and skills are not valued or welcomed. They feel they have lost their voice, that they are no longer seen as important, contributing members of the team. Feeling appreciated and valued is a key ingredient of trust and creates an environment of safety.

SAFETY LEADS TO TRUST

The frontiers of brain research continue to add gravitas to what self aware leaders instinctively know – when there are high levels of trust in a team there are far higher levels of collaboration, exploration and problem solving, not to mention happiness!

Brain imaging shows clearly that when we trust, the prefrontal cortex – the executive brain – floods with 'feel-good' chemicals such as oxytocin and dopamine. When this part of the brain is firing, it is responsible for growth, learning, connection, strategic thinking and problem solving. We feel safe to be vulnerable, to expose our thinking and test our assumptions. When we distrust, the amygdala – a part of the brain's emotional control system – closes down the secretion of the feel-good chemicals, causing us to feel uncertain, which can lead to a fear state. In this fear state the brain uses completely different sets of neural networks.

During distrust the chemicals flooding the brain, such as cortisol and norepinephrine, are more likely to induce negative thoughts, aggressive (or passive-aggressive) behaviour and survival mentality. We tend to jump to less-than-positive conclusions and 'bunker-down' our thinking. We no longer feel safe and we code people as 'foe' rather than 'friend'.

Leaders and team members I work with all see trust as paramount to the ability to deal with the complexity of the work, yet many are unsure about how to get out of a state of distrust in the first place. (If I distrust you, why should I ask you to trust me?) We get caught in a cycle of distrust, unwilling to be vulnerable and 'make the move'. We are also being held to ransom by our more primitive brain where the amygdala resides, becoming stressed, anxious and fearful.

Small steps – it doesn't take much to start the shift. Simply begin working with others in a way that honours you *and* them. Move away from 'I' thinking to 'we' thinking and start recoding those neural pathways from distrust to trust.

How does all this neuroscience fit with learning intelligence and the buzz?

As much as possible we want staff to be in a reward state to enable learning, problem solving, collaboration and innovation. When people are in a threat state, the behaviours you may observe include withdrawal, refusing to contribute and little or no learning. Innovation and risk-taking are avoided as safer options are chosen to minimise the threat.

I don't think it is hard to create a compelling, safe environment for adult learning. Everyone involved just needs to be more mindful about the creation and maintenance of it. We also need to take collective responsibility to do this.

Trust Building

Follow these five simple tips on how you can increase the trust within your teams as well as flood your own brain with the right kinds of chemistry!

1. Discover
Ask questions to discover more about what your people think and how they see the world.
Be genuinely curious to find out their opinions.

2. Appreciate
Notice and talk with your colleagues about what you appreciate about them.

3. Admit
Admit when you're wrong – and how you've learnt or are learning from it.

4. Evolve
Get rid of blame and justification language when you speak with others. Take responsibility for your actions and approaches.

5. Align
Do what you say you will do.

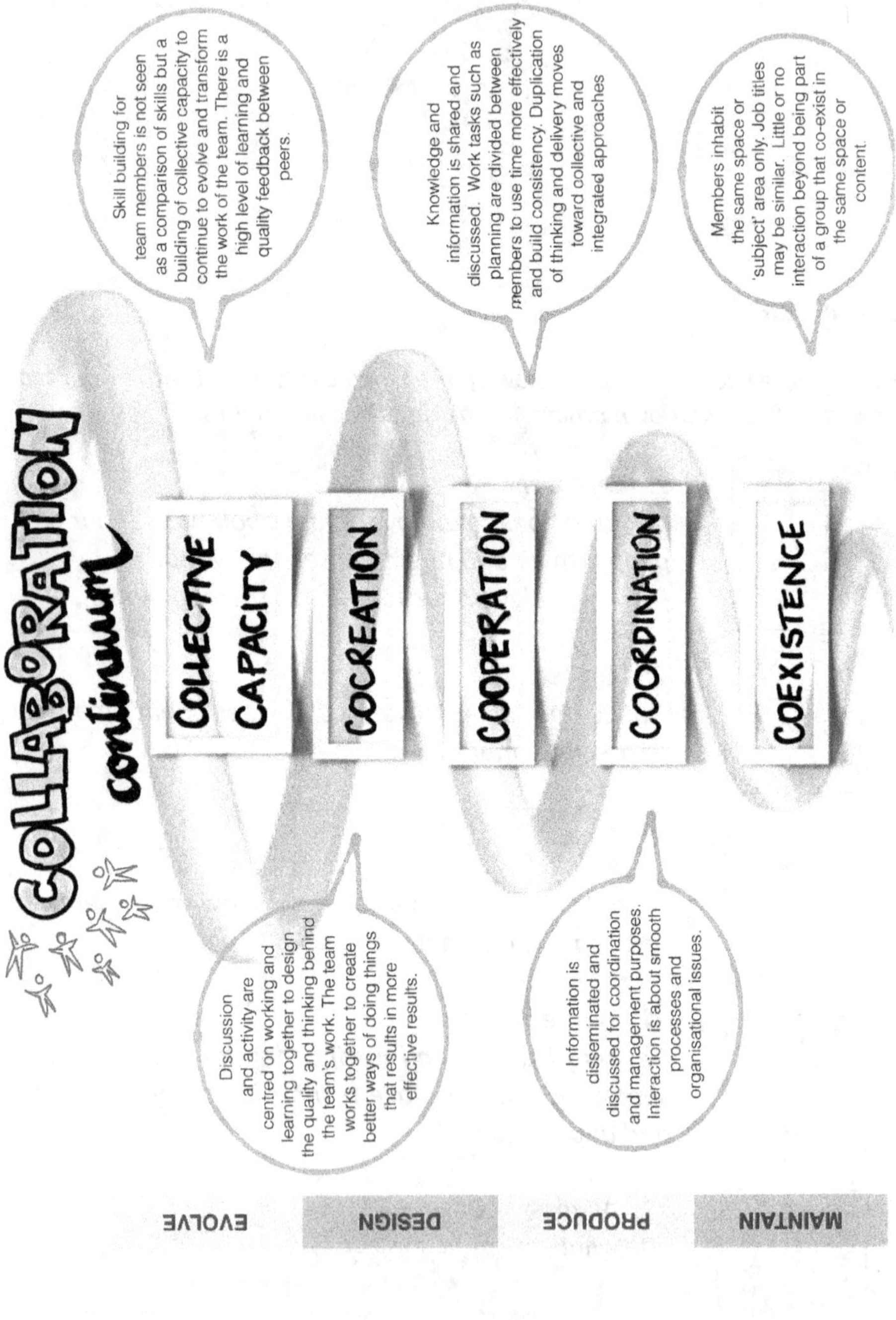

Collaboration Continuum

COLLECTIVE CAPACITY — Skill building for team members is not seen as a comparison of skills but a building of collective capacity to continue to evolve and transform the work of the team. There is a high level of learning and quality feedback between peers.

COCREATION — Discussion and activity are centred on working and learning together to design the quality and thinking behind the team's work. The team works together to create better ways of doing things that results in more effective results.

COOPERATION — Knowledge and information is shared and discussed. Work tasks such as planning are divided between members to use time more effectively and build consistency. Duplication of thinking and delivery moves toward collective and integrated approaches.

COORDINATION — Information is disseminated and discussed for coordination and management purposes. Interaction is about smooth processes and organisational issues.

COEXISTENCE — Members inhabit the same space or 'subject' area only. Job titles may be similar. Little or no interaction beyond being part of a group that co-exist in the same space or content.

- EVOLVE
- DESIGN
- PRODUCE
- MAINTAIN

Figure 7 – Collaboration Continuum

COMPELLING ENVIRONMENTS ARE COLLABORATIVE

Don't Mistake Coordination with Collaboration

Teachers with a rich professional development culture understand that collaboration doesn't just happen in meetings. Collaboration occurs in peer observation, peer feedback and critical observation when there is a teasing out of approaches and beliefs about student learning. There is collaboration when a number of people involved in a student's learning talk together and learn from each other about the best course of action to assist the student's growth and wellbeing. Collaboration is not just the sharing of knowledge; it is the creation of something more.

Figure 7 outlines a framework for you to assess how expansive your collaboration is. It ranges from co-existence through to collective capacity and shows where the underlying focus lies – is it to maintain the current state, to produce output, or to design and evolve practice?

See Roadblocks as Opportunity for Collaboration

Divergence of opinion and ideas is critical for new and inspiring ways of thinking and working. Professionals are given the opportunity to explore and reflect on past learning, their needs and possible future directions.

Sometimes in education we are too nice. There is often a preference to 'play nice', to maintain the surface harmony, so we put the perceived roadblocks in the too-hard basket. Growth mindset, however, guides us to believe that the greater the divergent, free-flowing thinking we can achieve in discussing and solving problems the more we learn. This helps us evolve our ways of thinking and working. Enabling this evolution requires processes that explore our perspectives and ideas, help us design and develop solutions, and clarify our future direction. We also need to see it as an opportunity rather than something to be avoided for the sake of harmony.

I remember reading an article years ago by a principal in an educational magazine asking the rhetorical question: 'Is there something not quite right about 500 teachers in an auditorium sitting and listening for a whole day about differentiating learning?' Often our default position in meetings is one person talking and directing the meeting, with everyone else listening.

It's a one-way, didactic interaction – a download of information that doesn't necessarily progress ideas or understanding. We don't do that in the classroom – or shouldn't – so why do we do it to ourselves as professional learners? Dynamic professional learning communities have a real *buzz* – the conversations are energetic, engaging and dynamic. The energy in the room crackles and the input is robust and empowering. People are asked critical questions and the emergent thinking is captured through various processes.

Trialing new ways of working in these times of increasing speed and complexity, requires us to be able to 'fail fast' and not see failure as a road block. To do this, we have to access feedback and evaluate as we go along. Just as we are moving to more formative assessment in the classroom, so too should we be testing our actions regularly, rather than waiting until the end of the implementation phase. A strong feedback loop through the 'design' process when working collaboratively or individually ties in with a flexible approach to trying innovative ideas.

CREATE YOUR OWN MASTER STOCK

If you are a lover of Asian foods, you may have eaten dishes created through the use of a master stock. A master stock is a luscious, rich concoction full of beautiful, aromatic spices and flavours lovingly brewed for a number of hours. Ingredients such as star anise, cassia bark, Szechuan peppers, garlic and ginger are put into a huge pot with soy, water and cooking wine. It is used for poaching meat or poultry.

The secret to the most amazing master stock is not to throw it out when it has been used, but to carefully store it and use it as the basis of the next master stock. After it has been used it is boiled, skimmed and strained, then cooled quickly. Some master stocks have been handed down through generations in this manner, leading to a depth of flavour that is seriously sublime!

A few years ago I had the good fortune to work for a number of years in my brother-in-law Teage's restaurant, as business manager. During this time I saw first hand how the chefs handled the master stock daily, adding more spice, aromatics and liquid. This master stock, which is the foundation of a number of the dishes the restaurant is famous for, was started when the restaurant opened 15 years ago. Teage's perspective on the master stock is that you have to get to know it to know how to improve it. The process requires patience and nurturing. He sees it as a living and working organism that never sleeps.

Collaboration in schools is like creating a master stock. The skills, experiences and 'school memory' of the staff who have been in the school for a long time are the foundation of the stock. For collaboration to be meaningful and fruitful there should be real valuing of what's gone before and how the journey of the school has created the *now*. But just as important, and adding to the complexity, is the addition of new staff, new experiences and expertise. Along with this comes new thinking by all involved. Artful leaders understand how to carefully and lovingly stir these into the existing culture and build the depth and strength of the professional community.

A wise group of teachers working through their collaborative practices in a workshop recently noted that just as it was crucial to know their students individually – to be providing high quality, targeted teaching and learning – it was also important to know each other in an expansive and deep way. This knowing leads to a more authentic use of each other's skills and taps into the beliefs driving their work together.

The other great quality about such a richness and depth to your professional learning group is that if you happen to add one wrong ingredient the strength of the others will make sure it doesn't affect the whole dish.

For collaboration to work, we need to believe that collaborating is a better than individuals plugging away at tasks on their own. If people collaborate on solving a shared problem or creating a new way of doing something, the solution is far more likely to succeed and the commitment to apply it will be more evident. Collaboration creates a wave of momentum that seeks to solve problems or simply find better ways to do those activities already being done well.

A synergy happens when people's voices are heard. Great ideas are picked up and piggy-backed on; there is a willingness to try, to see if something works, and a commitment as a group to monitor the effectiveness. Some assumptions that help with this belief are:

- People want to solve the problem

- There is goodwill in the room

- We have the right processes to get us to our desired outcomes.

Even though the assumptions might not be completely true at the outset, they allow for us to be on the lookout for behaviours that will help create the environment we are after.

COLLABORATIVE TOOLS

Excellent collaborative processes such as World Café and Open Space Technology are deliberatively designed to cut through the usual barriers to fruitful discussion. The way to use these dynamic processes is well documented on websites such as worldcafe.org, openspaceworld.org and in *Open Space Technology* by Harrison Owen. These processes set up groups to explore different opinions and approaches to issues, rather than seeing them as roadblocks.

World Café is based on asking critical and relevant open-ended questions, which are then explored by the group through a series of conversations. Open Space is more radical and is a process I love to be a part of. An over-arching question or statement is posed – for example, 'Our School in 2025' or 'How Do we Achieve our Vision?' The agenda for the time together is then created through individual people posting session discussions they'd like to explore and others signing up to come along. It is a free-flowing and emergent process that has amazing and surprising outcomes. There is ceremony to it and an honouring of all the participants in the room. In my experience it is not used much in education in Australia, which is a pity as it taps into the passions, energy and internal momentum of a group, which is so much more effective that than imposing a fixed agenda.

Visual Collaborative Tools

John Medina, in *Brain Rules: 12 Principles for Surviving and Thriving at Work, Home, and School*, talks about the ability of the brain to remember 65 per cent of information when it is presented with images and words, compared to a paltry 13 per cent with just words. Of his 12 principles for surviving and thriving, Rule No. 10 is *Vision trumps all senses*. Medina takes us through the way the brain uses visual receptors to make sense of the world. He also outlines the importance of visual input for memory:

> Put simply, the more visual the input becomes, the more likely it is to be recognized – and recalled. The phenomenon is so pervasive, it has been given its own name: the pictorial superiority effect, or PSE.

In the average team and staff meeting, how much time do you spend using visual language to help deepen the understanding or the learning? Imagine the shift simply by doing more of this. Infographics are a great example of capturing interesting information in a dynamic and engaging way. There are some great websites and apps templates for dropping in data and information to suit your needs. School resource areas are usually full of a range of thinking tools that can be used to guide and focus discussion and direction during professional dialogue.

In the Sir Ken Robinson *Changing Education Paradigms* YouTube video with RAS Animate, his speech is overlaid onto an animated visual journey that unfolds as he speaks. There have been over twelve-and-a-half million views of this clip, many of them to a room full of education staff. Graphic recording or facilitating in an education setting is always a hit. And for the record, if you're wondering, the Sir Ken Robinson animation was not done in real time, but created in the studio with a camera. The main point of course is the *impact* of this type of learning. It taps into the way our brains take on and retain information. Visual information remains in our memory for a far greater length of time than just words.

As a graphic facilitator I use visuals, either images or templates, to capture the learning while a group is working. The important parts of the discussion or learning models are caught and not passed by or avoided. Not only that, they are put up for all to see. This also means that important images and metaphors are used visually rather than just in speech. The infographic charts are often revisited in later sessions, which means the learning is not lost and the commitment to action is right in front of people.

Metaphors created by a group (e.g. the past three years have been like a steep road, but we are over the top of the mountain now; we're really taking off like a rocket, the momentum as grown so much) have extremely strong resonance and can enhance the language around a commitment to a course of action. The meaning a group attributes to a metaphor can unlock a very rich conversation in which deeper meaning and understanding is accessed and explored.

Asking a group or individual to 'tell me more' unearths perspectives not previously articulated and can open up a direction and flow that moves the group forward in a motivated and focused way. Some images and metaphors stay with staff groups for years, as they see them as a touchstone for a new direction in their journey.

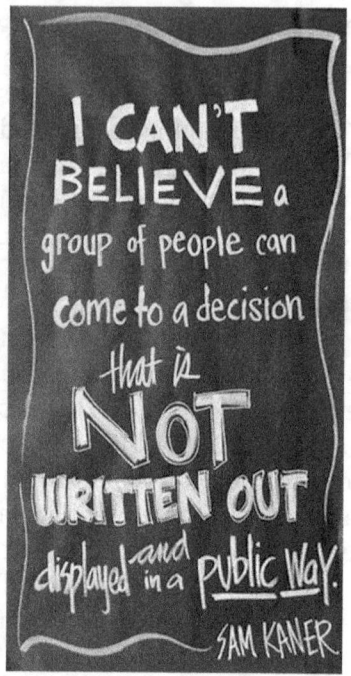

Figure 8 – Sam Kaner

Sam Kaner is a highly regarded facilitation expert who works globally with all types of groups. His perspective on public commitment is, 'I can't believe a group of people can come to a decision that is not written out and displayed in a public way'. The sign shown here was drawn by Lynn Carruthers, President of the International Forum of Visual Practitioners at the IFVP conference in New York in 2013. Large action plans and roadmaps showing the milestones for implementing new programs or initiatives on the staffroom wall remind everyone of what they have committed to.

Whenever I work with groups – small or large – I use visual collaborative tools. They're an easily created tool, especially in a school environment where paper, whiteboards and markers are within easy reach. So many teachers are incredibly creative, there is usually someone who will pick up a marker and start off.

COMPELLING ENVIRONMENT

Figure 9 – Why Work Visually?

Visuals also help simplify the complex. Often, while using large visual templates to capture discussion, a point arises when the whole group will 'see' exactly what they need to be focusing on, because it has come out so strongly through the process. This is especially true when great dialogue occurs through the process, allowing for patterns to emerge and deeper articulation of perspectives.

Visual collaborative tools help us move away from linear learning to integrative learning. They provide us with pointers to frame our thinking. Well-crafted questions then allow for positive, robust discussion. They give permission for strengths to be highlighted as well as challenges to be discussed in a useful, accountable way rather than a 'whinge-fest'.

Our need for strong collaboration to increase student outcomes has never been more pressing. Increasing complexity in the world demands that we be more innovative in the way we work and mindful that the way we work is having an impact on student outcomes. We need to be relentless in our pursuit of finding engaging and deeply explorative ways to discuss, dream, design and plan what we do in schools.

A Note on PowerPoint Purgatory

Picture a room full of people waiting to be illuminated by the expert at the front of the room. The expert starts speaking by launching into a detailed analysis of their favourite subject, turning at a 45-degree angle between the audience and the screen. Up on the screen are slides and slides of ... words ... in 22-point font (or less, 'cos there's so much to fit in!). The presenter's head turns further towards the screen to read. Ten slides later, up pops a graph ('Woo hoo,' you think. 'A picture!'). But, no. The expert says: 'I know you can't read this, but it basically says ... ' and the droning continues.

> **A Message For Presenters** ↗
> (from those who are suffering)
>
> ## Powerpoint Purgatory
>
> 1. Generally, in a room full of educators, everyone can read
> 2. I came to hear *you,* dear expert, not read your information on a slide.
> 3. If you put stuff up – make sure people can SEE IT!
> 4. I want to be *engaged* and *stimulated* by your presentation – not bored to snores..........

What a waste! If you *have* to use PowerPoint, use it to engage. Use meaningful visuals and impactful segues in your presentation. We are becoming more and more enlightened as to how to use PowerPoint effectively. Steve Jobs was an expert, and there are many other useful examples. TED Talks are a great way to see highly effective use of PowerPoint or Keynote. Seth Godin and Malcolm Gladwell use them particularly well.

Donna McGeorge, an expert in training educators and trainers in facilitating dynamic sessions, has written a book called *The Pen Is Mightier Than The Slide* in which she talks about the opportunity to use flip charts and visuals to co-create with the people in the room. The title says it all about the main idea of the book. If you are addicted to PowerPoint, see donnamcgeorge.com for a dose of inspiration.

Graphic Recording

Another visual dimension of my work that I love is graphic recording. I stand at the side or back of a room and 'record' the essence of a speaker's presentation or the discussion in the room. Not recording with a microphone, but drawing and writing on a large sheet of paper. The idea is that I capture the main points and 'a-ha' moments in the room in a visual, dynamic and engaging way. The thing I love most about recording is the number of people who come up and say, 'Oh, that is just how I learn best. You've captured what I heard.'

I was privileged to graphically record John Medina when he was the keynote speaker at the Australia Council of Educational Leaders (ACEL) national conference in 2014 in Melbourne. He was speaking on bringing the science of learning together with the practice of learning. He has a strong message for increased learning. He presented research and, in his inimitable, fabulous, gregarious style, told us to, 'Get off your backside and exercise more'. (YouTube him if you haven't seen him – he has highly relevant research and approaches and his book is very pertinent for educators.)

Research shows that exercise impacts our executive function, particularly the self-regulation and cognitive control area of our brain. Exercise is one of the biggest indicators of success in learning, business and life. If you want to see his presentation as a graphic chart, done in real time on the stage as John was presenting, go to my website: traceyezard.com.

I have worked with a number of schools that have started graphically capturing whatever is being presented to them. Many teachers have jumped at the chance to use colour and form to represent the ideas in a different way from just using ballpoint and lists. One of my colleagues in the US, Lynn Kearny, calls using visuals 'increasing the size of the mental desktop'. Let's face it, with life as fast and complex as it is, any help is gratefully accepted.

Figure 10 gives an example of the capture of a keynote address by Richard Gerver talking on edupreneurship at the ACEL national conference.

Figure 10 – Richard Gerver, ACEL Conference 2014

More Tools

On the following pages are a few examples of collaborative tools you can use to add to well known tools such as a PMI (plus, minus, interesting) chart, De Bono's Thinking Hats and SWOT analysis. When you look at them, you will notice at least one thing. They are incredibly simple yet serve to take the discussion and reflection deeper than the surface issues we often get caught up in. The tools can also provide a process to guide you through the discussion rather than meandering all over the place. You can use them A3 size on a table, or on the wall or whiteboard large scale. Use your professional judgment when deciding whether to have smaller or large group discussions, or a combination.

Journey Map

Use this as a fun way to share the story of the school in small groups. Put the maps up on the walls and do a gallery walk around them at the end to discuss differing perspectives, key events, major themes. Print them on A2 or bigger, or draw them yourself on large paper. Encourage further discussion and reflection. This process is also a great one to use with your community.

Critical Incident Management Flowchart

This is an example of how you can map an issue to plan your approach. Any major issue can be put at the top and the headings stay the same or are modified, depending on what you want out of the conversation. 'Present state' allows you to discuss with your team the realities of the now with the 'desired state' being the place to capture what would be in evidence if you reached your vision.

Me – Building Connection

Use this in a newly formed team situation to deepen understanding, empathy and knowledge of skills and motivation. Every person creates a large poster of themselves with the headings listed (images encouraged!). Individuals then share this with the group. The group asks questions of the individual that further unpack the chart. This activity is also great for getting people to value each other more and appreciate skills.

Design Thinking

This basic template is simply about bringing people's thinking into the light and articulating it clearly through the ideation process. It can be used individually, in small groups or as a large template. Include words and images. There is nothing rocket science-y about this approach – just a way for us to look at our thoughts and reflect more creatively and collaboratively.

Project Planning

This template allows everyone to see at a glance the purpose of your project, who's involved and your key steps. Create this large scale as a blank canvas and co-create your plan together. Keep it visible during the project; add comments and insights along the way to keep it living.

TeamManifesto

This is an example of another approach to team protocols. I find the discussion that goes into these types of documentation far richer than a list of boring 'we wills...'

THE BUZZ

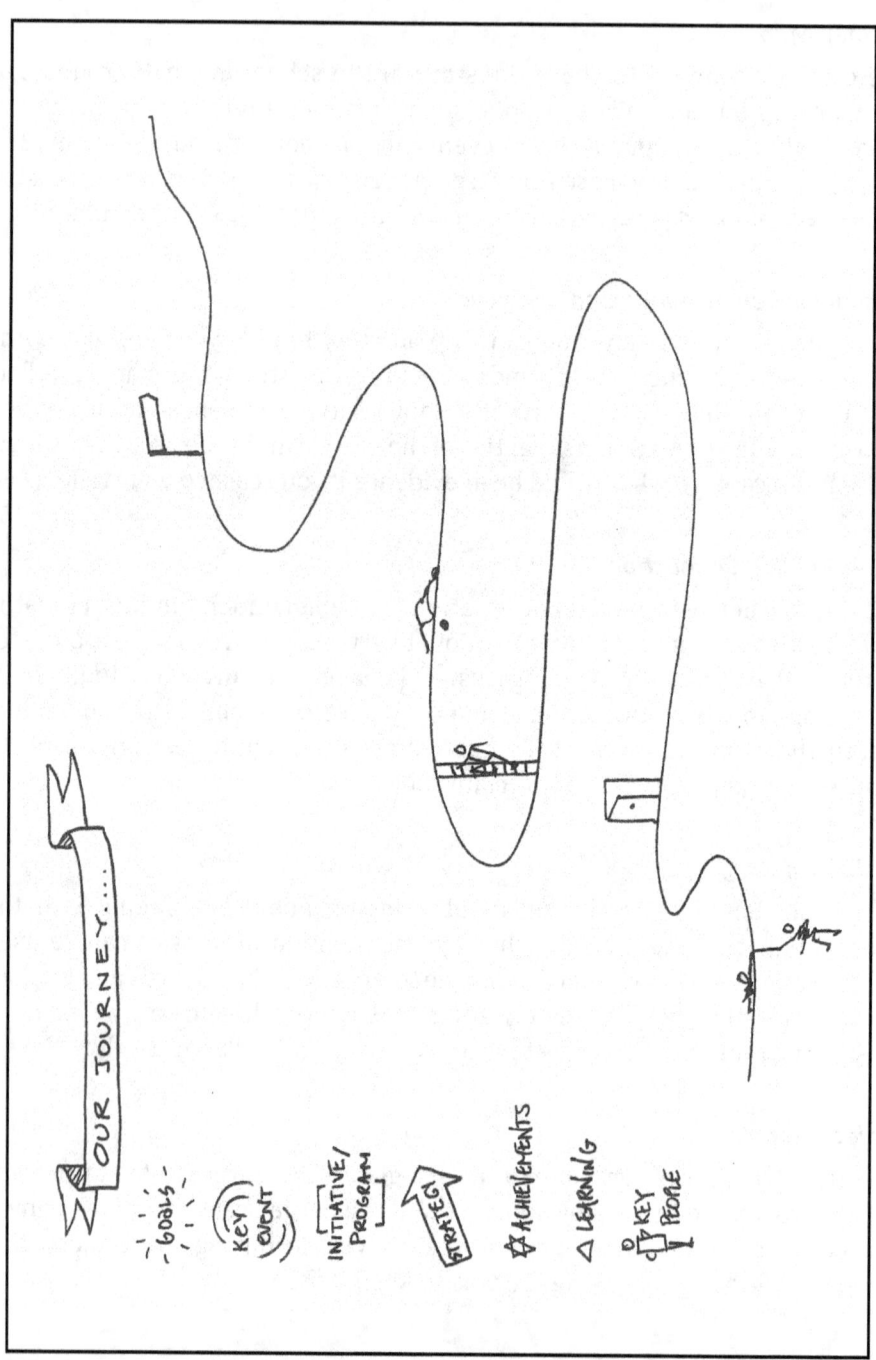

Figure 11 – Journey Map

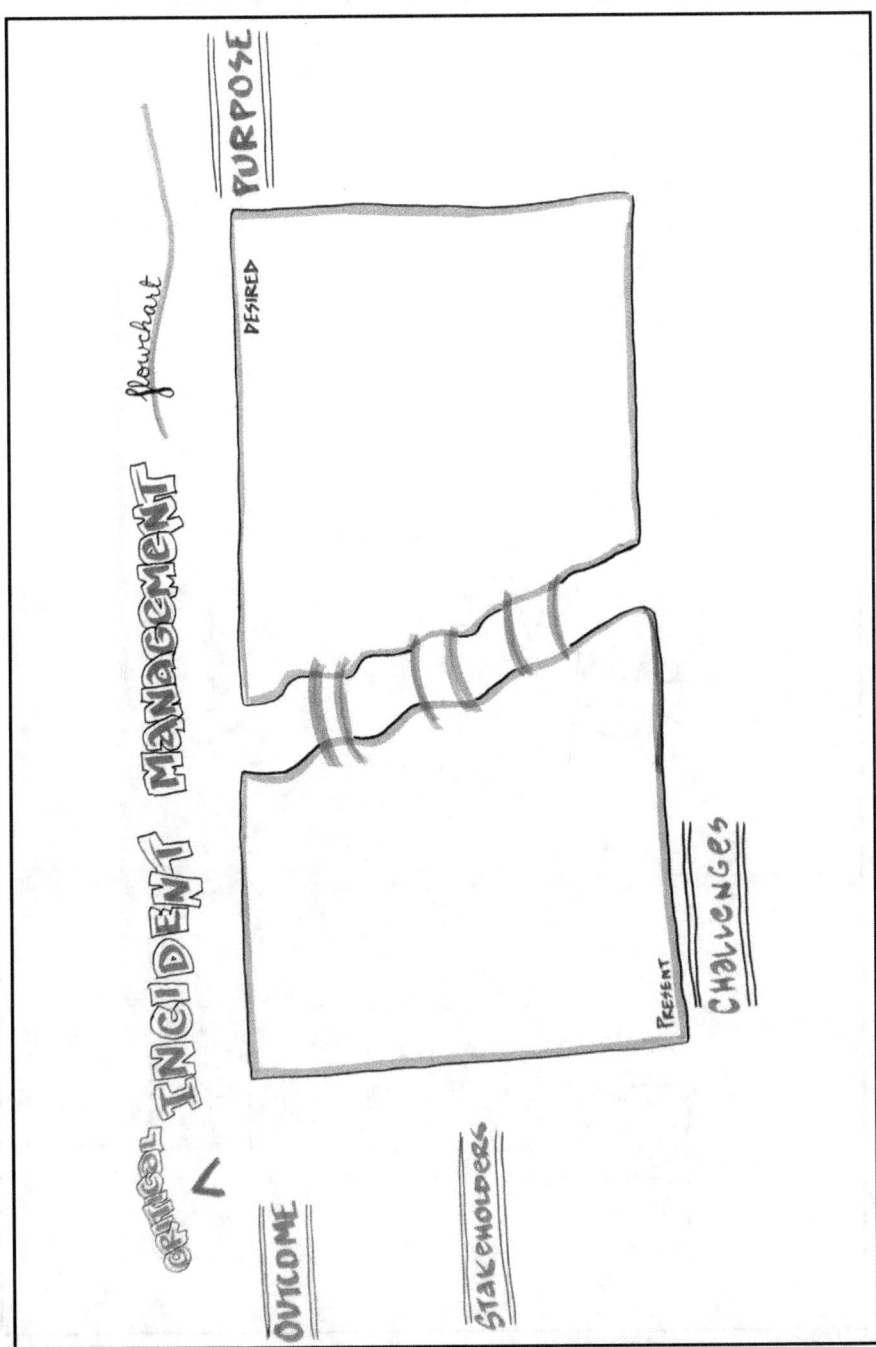

Figure 12– Critical Incident

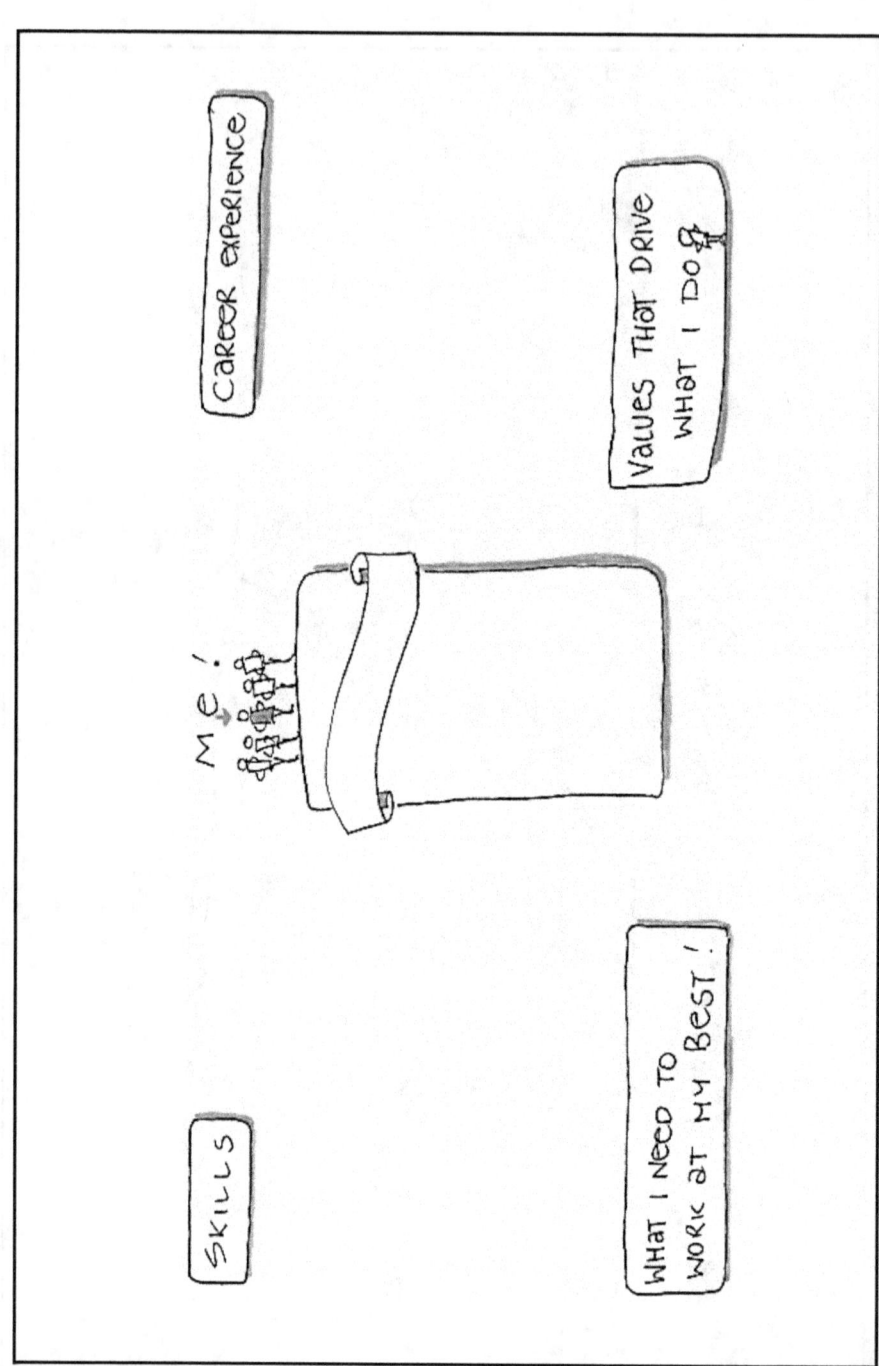

Figure 13 – Me

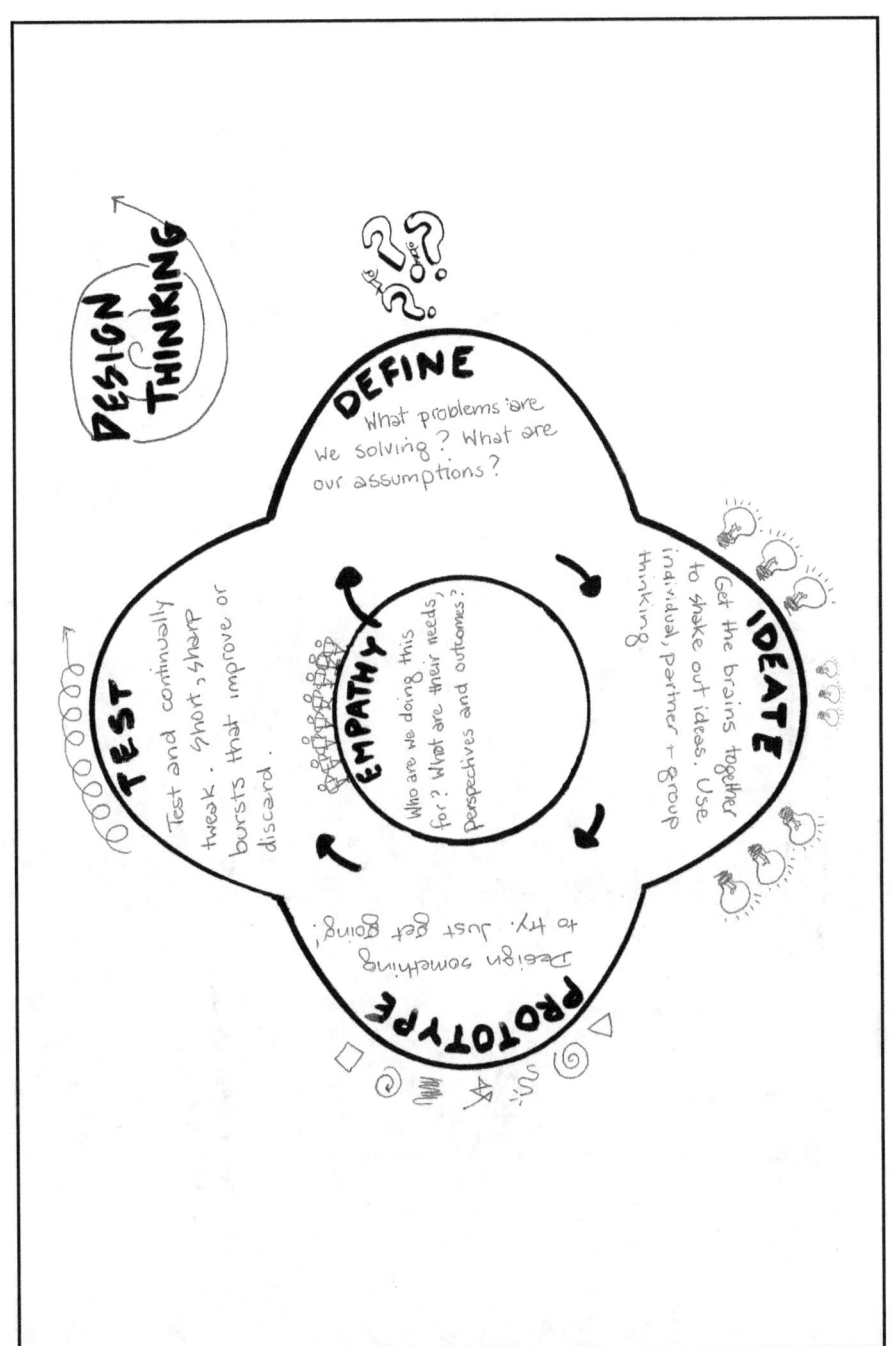

Figure 14 – Design Thinking

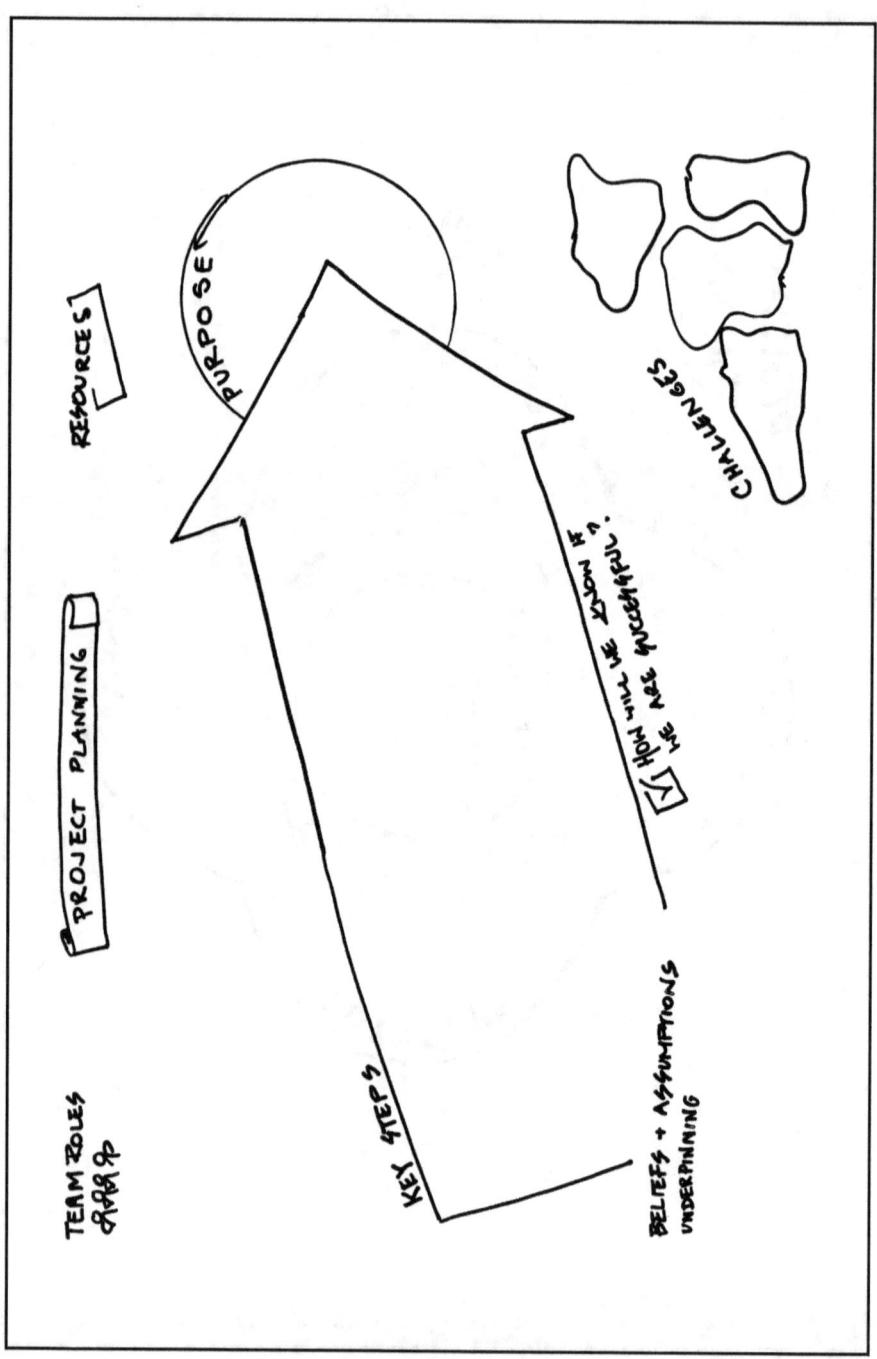

Figure 15 – Project Planning

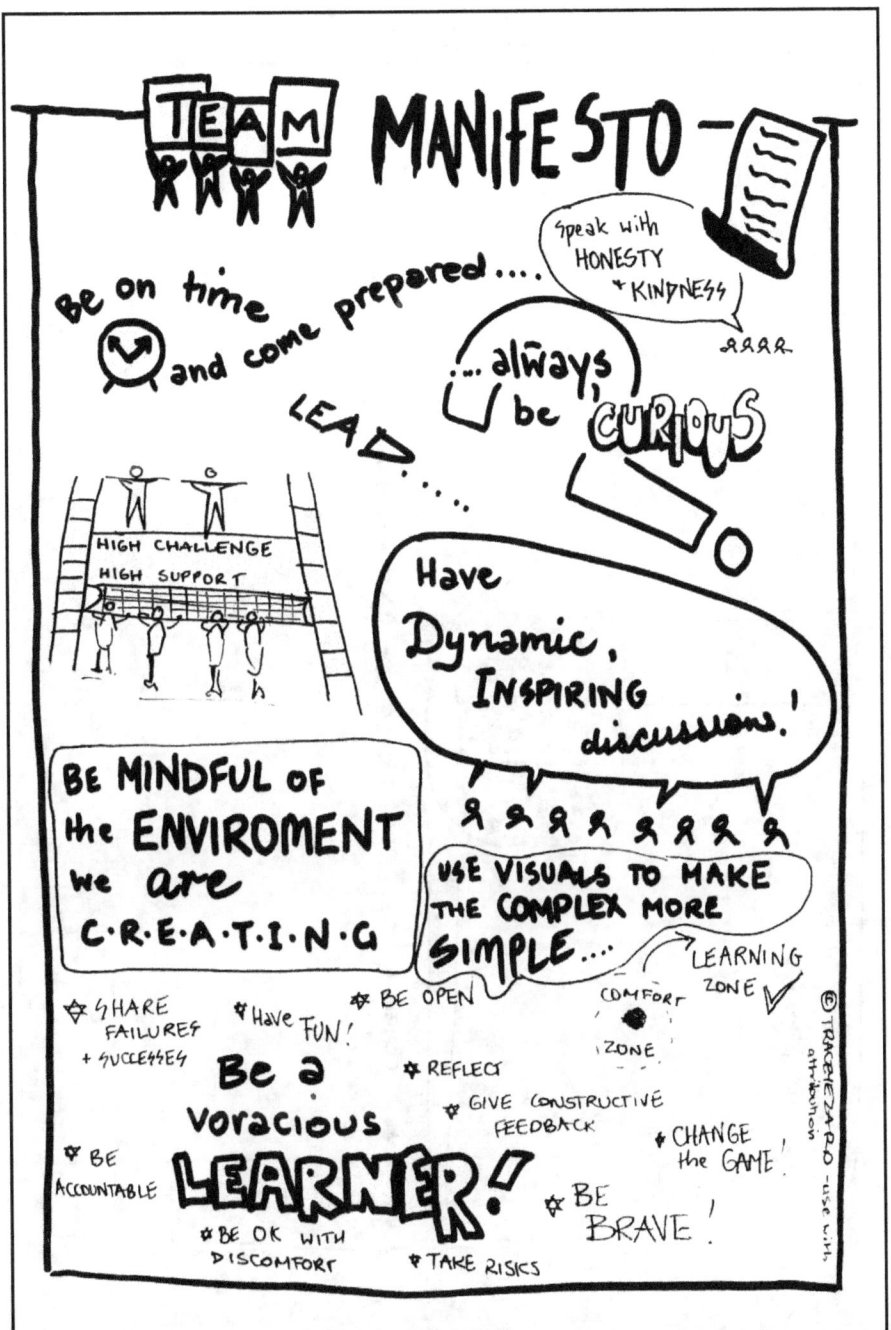

Figure 16 – Team Manifesto

Figure 17 – Team Agreement

SHAKE IT UP – COMPELLING ENVIRONMENTS HAVE VARIETY

How many meetings have you been stuck in that you either felt like throwing something in frustration or falling asleep through boredom?

Meetings don't need to be boring or frustrating but will continue to be unless they are run differently. Meetings in schools with the buzz are different for a whole range of reasons sprinkled throughout this book. There are so many easy ways to keep your colleagues awake and engaged. Here are some:

Doodle

The action of doodling is incredibly inspiring for many people. Encourage it by putting out paper and coloured textas. Research has shown that people who doodle when they are listening are more able to recall the information they are listening to. If you are a doodler, I am sure you have been at the receiving end of a withering look from the person running the meeting. Doodle on! I say. And perhaps educate them as to the latest research that shows you are taking in perhaps even more information than others.

Many teachers love colour and love having a marker in their hands. It's a great way to mix up a meeting or session. It's inspiring when people who love making models or metaphors get a hold of a good bunch of coloured markers.

Move

Use the kinaesthetic mode. Get up and work together on the walls or on the tables (on paper or whiteboards!). If you have a difficult issue to tease out, go for a wander around the school and school grounds in pairs or threes for 10 minutes, discussing it and coming back with your thoughts ready to be articulated. If it's a beautiful day, have your meeting outside.

Engage your Brain

Juggling balls are a great way to get your brain going when it's stuck. Brain Gym is another great way to get the neurons moving. One of my favourites to get people's brains moving is to get them to stand, put their left foot out in the air slightly, and raise their left hand. I get them to draw a six from the top in the air with their hand and then

turn their foot in a clockwise direction. It's a bit like rubbing your stomach in a circle while tapping your head, but more fun. This just helps to shake things up a bit and generally increases the resourcefulness in the room if the energy is a bit low.

Use the Space

Use the space and the bodies in the room to indicate levels of agreement or commitment. Here's an example:

'Let's make a physical line in the room – put yourself on the end if you feel completely ready to go ahead with this direction, in the middle if you still need some convincing or at the start if you are dead against it.'

Then have a great discussion about where everyone is at. I find that people have quite deep, powerful and transparent discussions when they are standing and articulating the reasons for their positions – and there is a distinct amount of trust and honesty displayed. For some reason the energy standing and discussing in an informal way helps to create the safety for exploration.

I was running a leadership program in a secondary school a few years ago. After a few sessions we moved out of our usual classroom, which was in the flexible-learning Year 7 space, into another part of the school.

As we walked in, the tables were set up in this configuration shown in Figure 18.

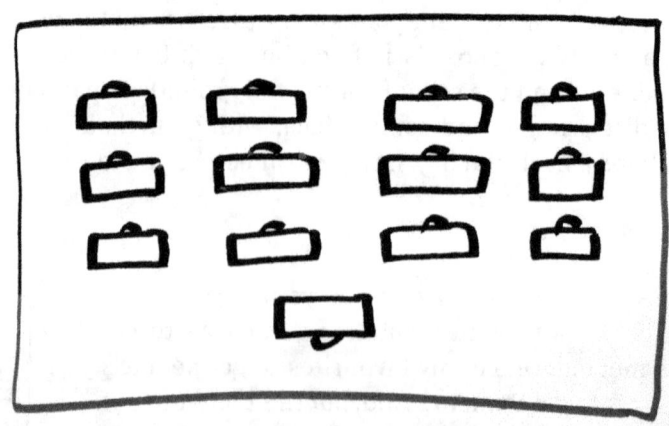

Figure 18 – Conducive to Collaborative Learning?

Thinking the room was set up for some pretty head-down, individual skill- or concept-based learning or reflection, I started moving the tables for the usual group configuration. One of the teachers said, 'This is still set up from the regular maths faculty meeting'.

I was a bit gobsmacked! Apparently the maths faculty head always wanted it set up this way. He would come in and sit at the front, facing everyone, speak at them, ask infrequent, closed questions (and probably wonder why there was not a lot of input) and then move to the next point. Some of the faculty members sat up the back on their laptops doing work – or something. The diagram of the table setup shown is not conducive to strong collaborative or robust discussion! And I bet there was little or none of that going on.

It would be really interesting to unpack the mindset and beliefs the faculty head has about professional, collegiate learning. In your own setups, have another look at the space then think about how to create a collaborative, thriving, professional team. Go from there.

Changing the Environment

When it comes to changing the environment for your meetings, there are a few easy things to put in place:

- *Move venues*

    Use places that will encourage questions about learning in that space – it's a great dialogue enhancer. Don't get stuck holding it in the team leader or faculty head's space. Go to the local coffee shop for an early-morning meeting or after school.

- *Set up*

    Set up the furniture so you can easily converse in a non-hierarchical manner.

- *Bring food!*

    After a long day of teaching, a pick-me-up is always good. Try for nutritious snacks rather than a sugar fest, though. Sugary foods tend to leave you wanting in 30 minutes or so.

- *Processes*

    Get people working in smaller groups or encourage thinking by using processes like 'Think. Pair. Share.' See suggestions for collaborative processes in this section to get some more ideas.

Processes for Agendas

- *Look at your agenda. If you have stuck with the same agenda for a while, it may be getting stuck, predictable and comfortable. Mix it up.*

- *If your meetings are full of administrivia, get rid of as much of it as you can. Use technology, whiteboards or bulletins to exchange static information and keep as much time as possible clear for dialogue.*

- *Be clear with each other as to items that require all-in discussion and those a team member can be responsible for. If your team tends to want to have a hand in every decision, chances are you are exerting too much energy in this space. We need to trust our colleagues and let them make decisions. Not all decisions need to be collaborative or by committee. This leads to paralysis and a sense of frustration.*

- *Have different people run the meetings.*

- *Use a variety of modes such as visual, auditory, kinaesthetic. It doesn't have to be full on, just a regular occurrence.*

- *Discuss meeting protocols at the start of the school year. I'm not a stickler for this one – some groups have the ability to work fabulously together without protocol. You know your team – use your judgment. If some people aren't clear on professional expectations then it may be wise to use protocols. Another approach is to create a commitment code or team manifesto – a way to capture a rich discussion about what we expect of each other.*

    o *Be clear on purpose.*

- Encourage time when you don't use tablets or laptops, especially when you are having a rigorous debate. Decide as a group how you will use technology.

- Set up beliefs about what is important to you as a group and how you turn up when you come to meetings, as well as your higher purpose.

AITSL Frameworks

The Australian Institute of Teaching and School Leadership (AITSL) has been instrumental in helping schools focus on building the learning intelligence of staff to increase teaching quality through the creation of national standards and frameworks. AITSL was formed as a commitment of the state and federal governments to promote excellence in the profession of teaching and school leadership and is funded by the Commonwealth. AITSL's focus is on practicing teachers and principals, and initial teacher education. Its theory of action is knowledge + commitment = effective implementation.

AITSL has rigorously co-created these frameworks and standards in conjunction with educators throughout Australia. A huge amount of consultation and co-creation has helped to design and continue to develop high quality support for systems, schools and teachers.

The website has access to many tools that will help create a plan for building your professional learning. There are frameworks and tools for observation and evaluation, professional learning, self-assessment and coaching. It also has great resources to increase your collaborative learning processes. There are links to design-thinking tools for educators. One I particularly recommend to help ideate, design and experience things using a variety of modes is 'Bootcamp Bootleg'.

5. AUTHENTIC DIALOGUE

When the professional learning community in a school is focused on improving quality teaching and learning, the educational literature tells us that we can really impact what is happening in the classroom. Continually improving authentic dialogue that is rigorously and unashamedly based on collaborative teaching and learning in the classroom is the main game. Respectful, dynamic and exciting conversations between educators – always focused on learning how to provide the highest standard of teaching and learning for students – are contagious.

Parry Graham in his 2007 article, 'The Role of Conversation, Contention, and Commitment in a Professional Learning Community, poses:

> One of the first steps that a school leader needs to take in creating a professional learning community is to encourage purposeful conversations. Modeling these types of conversations is one strategy in this direction; a leader who actively engages others in purposeful dialogue focused around teaching and learning sends a message that this type of dialogue is important and valued. Another strategy is to set organisational expectations that encourage, or even require, purposeful conversations.

Leadership Team Reflection

1. *What modeling of authentic, purposeful conversations is your leadership team contributing to and leading? Take some time to reflect as a leadership team on your own conversations.*

2. *Is there a clear vision for who you are and what you stand for?*

3. *What are your assumptions of each other and your roles in leading the school?*

4. *Whatever the leadership structure in your school, are you certain how you lead it?*

5. *Are you all clear on your collective goals and the outcomes you want? Have you asked yourselves: what does success look like in our school?*

These authentic dialogue conversations can be a watershed moment in the life of a school on the journey to improvement.

NEVER ASSUME – PURPOSEFUL DIALOGUE

CASE STUDY

As the principal of Warracknabeal Secondary, Tony Fowler was committed to challenging assumptions in his school and increasing conversations about teaching and learning. He and his staff rigorously peeled back the layers of their assumptions about students, including their abilities, what works and what hasn't worked, pedagogy and behaviour management.

Fowler's focus for the school was to build the strength of the professional learning community and leadership, and use the Curiosity and Powerful Learning (CPL) strategy for school improvement. CPL is based on building instructional and leadership capacity. It focuses on leaders promoting and participating in professional learning that enhances teacher capacity, while reducing variation within schools.

The school's dialogue has become focused on teaching, learning and multiple feedback sources and is yielding great improvement in organisational climate. As a result, responses on student and staff surveys have improved in all areas.

In the three years that the school has been on this journey, it has achieved great improvement in student learning outcomes. This has included achievement in a number of their cohorts to more than twice the expected level of growth in numeracy and three times the expected level in writing.

Fowler and his team have been relentless in their focus on creating a collaborative professional learning community where informal and formal discussions about teaching and learning are the norm. An important part of their discussions has been to unpack their assumptions.

When I was a kid, my dad designed and set up one of the first electronic security control rooms, which controlled back-to-base alarms. It was a big deal. Electronic security was in its infancy, and my dad was one of the pioneers of the technology and systems. I loved hanging out in the control room.

There were screens everywhere showing camera views, and ... computers! I'm talking the late 1970s here. It was a magical thing to be able to sit at a screen and, using MSDOS (no Windows or iOS back then), play *Colossal Cave Adventure*, which was a kind of precursor to *Dungeons and Dragons*. There were no graphics, you just typed in commands and had to make it to the treasure before you were eaten by a troll or killed by a knife-throwing dwarf. The game had to be given explicit commands: 'Turn left at the rock'. One bad command and you were dead. You got feedback straight away. The next line would tell you exactly what happened when your command had been executed.

The computer made only one assumption: exactly what you said should be done would be done. There was no grey and no 'sort of, kind of, maybe'. Binary response = success or failure. After a while, we were able to learn the commands needed and the responses they'd bring – our assumptions became beliefs as we got more experience with different commands. I knew that if I picked up the knife at a certain point in the game I would then have it to kill the dwarf around the corner of the next rock.

But as soon as we put the human element into play, assumptions rule our world. Grey is everywhere. Ambiguity and uncertainty are more prevalent than ever before. Working with a huge range of people, one of the joys in my job is tapping into the divergent thinking, and understanding people's perceptions more.

The challenge of strong collaborative communities is to understand the assumptions being made, then articulate them, examine them and test them. It takes time, but the clarity that comes from those discussions leads to greater levels of understanding, empathy and alignment.

Funnily enough, the *standing order manual* that Dad wrote and had in his control room started out with this line on the first page:

Standing Order Number One – Never Assume.

DOUBLE-LOOP LEARNING

One of the strategies that Tony Fowler and the team at Warracknabeal Secondary College use as part of the Curiosity and Powerful Learning approach is to revisit their assumptions through application of the Double-Loop Learning model. He used this double-loop learning model to relay the way they have gone about things differently.

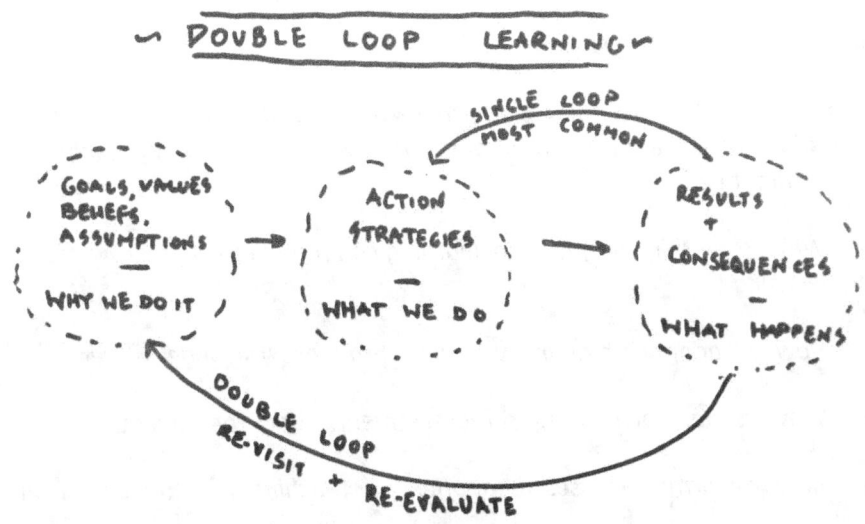

Figure 19 – Double Loop Learning

The Double-Loop Learning Model was coined by Professor Chris Argyris, a global leader in business theories of change and organisational development. It is outlined thoroughly in Peter Senge's *The Fifth Discipline Fieldbook*. Argyris was a Professor Emeritus at Harvard Business School and gave the world some of the best thinking around assumptions and learning. Double-Loop Learning shows us that to solve complex problems and continually improve, we need to get beyond simply 'problem solving'. This model reveals the importance of the mindset aspect of learning intelligence. It's about looking beneath what we do or have done to ask why we are doing it. Argyris calls this part of the learning loop the 'theory of action'.

Testing Assumptions Part A

1. *List some of the assumptions you make that you should test. Some simple questions to tease out assumptions and have authentic dialogue about an issue might be:*

    - *Why do we think professional learning communities will improve student learning?*

    - *How will adopting a genre-writing program grow stronger writers?*

    - *Why are we implementing self-assessment rubrics for students?*

    - *How will formative assessment affect our teaching and student learning?*

It makes sense to carefully think through the decisions you are making by articulating publicly – with authentic dialogue – the rationale being used and checking the assumptions being made.

THE LADDER OF INFERENCE

Another useful model for testing our beliefs explicitly through dialogue again comes from Professor Argyris: the Ladder of Inference.

The model takes us up the stages we go through to reach a belief, which then drives our actions. The less attractive part of this in humans is when we jump very quickly to an erroneous belief that harms ourselves or others. This sometimes occurs in the blink of the eye – our brain has received a scrap of information that has us leaping to wild and/or fixed assumptions.

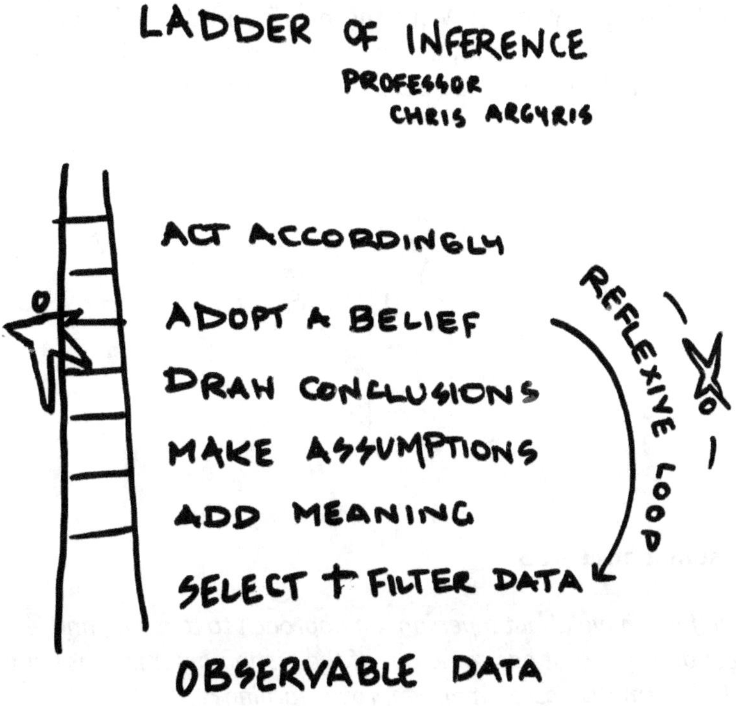

Ladder of Inference
Professor Chris Argyris

- Act Accordingly
- Adopt a Belief
- Draw Conclusions
- Make Assumptions
- Add Meaning
- Select + Filter Data
- Observable Data

Reflexive Loop

Figure 20 – Ladder of Inference

Helping us to become aware of these assumptions, the Ladder of Inference model alerts us to the dangers of this *reflexive loop*.

Sometimes we have such fixed beliefs that we only track for data that *supports* those beliefs. The beauty of this model is that it can remind us to test our assumptions. Usually they are something we do not question because they're so aligned with our beliefs we don't test them out.

Stephen Covey, in his worldwide bestseller, *The 7 Habits of Highly Effective People*, tells the story of being in the New York subway one Sunday afternoon when a man and his noisy children burst into the carriage and totally changed the quiet dynamic in the train. While the man sat silently next to Stephen, the children ran amok. After a time of people becoming increasingly frustrated with the children, Stephen mentioned quietly to the man that he thought the children were upsetting people on the train. The man woke up as out of a reverie, mentioned that they had come from the hospital where his wife had just died, and that he and the children didn't know how to handle it.

Stephen Covey called it a 'mini paradigm shift'. It is a poignant example of the Ladder of Inference in action. With the newfound data, the people on the train were able to access compassion and empathy for the father and the children, where before there had been a growing frustration.

Testing Assumptions Part B

Take a belief *you have about a person, an approach to teaching and learning, or perhaps a statement that has come out of the testing-assumptions activity, such as: How does formative assessment improve learning?*

Examine the belief. *How does it drive your behaviour? Walk yourself down the ladder from the belief. Where does that belief come from? From what data have you drawn your conclusions? What assumptions have you made? How much observable data do you have that supports the belief? Is there any other data you could access to really check and track your belief around it?*

EXPLICIT EXPECTATIONS

Many misunderstandings between colleagues arise as a result of assumptions in expectations. Rather than avoid explicit discussions about expectations of each other, thriving collaborative teams clarify acceptable team behaviours and accountability. Roles and responsibilities are clear and the direction and vision of the team is articulated and committed to. Figure 16 on page 89 is an example of a team manifesto that demonstrates how some of these conversations may result.

SLAY THE ELEPHANTS IN THE ROOM

A bit violent perhaps, but how many initiatives get blocked because people are not actually talking about the issue? By nature we tend to avoid the difficult. Think of all the sayings we have to support avoidance: 'Don't open that can of worms' and 'It's the elephant in the room' or 'We know why this will never happen, don't we?' There is a particular energy in a room that is held to ransom by the unsaid. People shift in their seats, break eye contact, or look to other members with a knowing glance. Some don't say a word. Others express their comments in the corridor after the meeting.

QUESTIONS, QUESTIONS, QUESTIONS

To create a thriving learning community we need to be obsessed with questions and then listen keenly to the answers. There is magic when an essential question is asked with layers of perspectives and ideas being explored.

Arm yourself with some great questions before a meeting or crucial conversation. Or simply be more mindful about asking open, explorative questions to create dialogue that is designed to explore rather than close, finalise, shut down or avoid.

What questions do you ask the group you are working with beyond the knowledge level of Bloom's Taxonomy? How do you get comprehension, application, analysis, synthesis and evaluation? These levels are used constantly from a teaching point of view; we should also be using them from a teacher point of view. Perhaps in your compelling environment you put up some of the more complex questions on the walls to encourage deeper questions and help grow the learning intelligence.

In general, we know that open-ended questions are the key to authentic two-way dialogue. Past- and present-type questions I call backward-facing questions. (e.g. What did? How does?) Future-facing questions lead us to thinking about what comes next or further in the future. We are exploring our thinking and imagining what could be. (Where could? Who might? What will?)

Encourage discussion leaders to be judicious in their choice of backward-facing questions. Present and past tense questioning can lead to being stuck in blames and justifications if we are not careful. While carefully analysing occurrences and learnings is important, we need to know when to turn our faces towards the future. What will we do next time? What might it look like if we do it again? Where will we make the most change? Looking forward to possibility and through to imagination significantly points us towards the future – and the future is sometimes a far more optimistic and action-oriented place to focus.

When we have a growth mindset, questions about the past and future tap into wonder and curiosity, as well as possibility and learning. They allow us to delve into the past, reflecting on what was learnt and how it can inform our future. When our mindset is fixed, both the past and the future can bring fear and a strong anchor to the 'way things were before'.

Listening to the types of questions we ask ourselves and each other can give great insight into the space we are coming from – one of possibility and new thinking, or status quo and same thinking.

Exploring through Questioning

1. The key to exploration is great questioning. Ask probing questions to reflect on the past. It allows for the flow of the conversation to be explorative, expansive and non-judgmental. Use questions such as:

   - *What were the reasons behind that decision?*
   - *What learning came out of that experience?*
   - *Did anyone else have a different perspective on that situation?*

2. Questions that look to the future should challenge, yet assume possibility and opportunity:

   - *What's the most important priority for us straight away?*
   - *Out of all of these options, which is most closely aligned to what we think would most benefit to this group of students?*
   - *How are we giving the students a voice in this decision process?*
   - *What will we need to be mindful of as we implement this across the school?*
   - *What does our community expect of us?*

The Five Whys

There are lots of clever ways in which process-driven organisations delve into their challenges to find the cause of the issue. Root cause analysis is one such approach that originated in the more mechanical world of manufacturing, engineering and similar industries. It has useful application when clear and logical analysis is required. However, the premise can still help us have authentic dialogue that searches for the real cause rather than symptoms. Therefore the solution can be found and applied at the level the problem exists, rather than at the consequences of that problem. Often these 'consequences' are blamed for far more than they should be. Each step of the why needs to be grounded in fact before you move on.

CASE STUDY – The FIVE WHYS

At a workshop I was running with a school in review time – exploring where they had been and where they were heading – we were having an in-depth conversation about what they needed to *let go of*. Much of what was happening in the school occurred because 'That's what we've always done' or 'Susan's been running that program for years and we are all really attached to it'.

One group was exploring how they could simplify the timetable to gain streamlined time for the curriculum rather than 'stuff'. One of the grade teachers said, 'We need to change choir time out of the timetable into a lunchtime.'

Why do we need to change choir time?

Because we don't have enough class time with our students.

Why don't we have enough class time with our students?

They are often out with specialists and when we do get them, some are still out at special programs.

Why are they often out with specialists?

We were given an extra hour allocation to put peer observation in place a couple of years ago via the specialist program.

Why are you given that amount of preparation time?

It was to support us trying something new in our professional growth.

Why is this support still in place?

We haven't reviewed or evaluated the peer observation program to understand whether the support is still needed.

After more in-depth discussion, it was clear to everyone that the amount of preparation time was no longer required, as the staff were committed to using a certain number of hours per term to continue their development in this area. In actual fact, choir was not the issue regarding the lack of contact time, it was a more random consequence of not reviewing something that had been put in place and was now not needed.

Don't Just Listen for the Gap

Of course, clever questioning has to be coupled with clever listening. When we are talking about something around which there are a number of high stakes, often the default position is to simply listen for the gap rather than carefully and mindfully understanding what the person is saying then asking clarifying questions, or linking what they are saying to the way we see things. Not hearing people and just jumping into the gap with our questions can be a blind spot in our unconscious competence. Mindfully listening can actually be a hard habit to catch!

INCREASING DIALOGUE THROUGH STORYTELLING

Personal Storytelling

Storytelling is a powerful way of sharing perspectives and increasing our understanding of each other. If you are leading any type of collaborative work, artful storytelling is a powerful way of using auditory learning to its greatest advantage. One of my favourite things to do with a bunch of teachers just back from holidays is to get them telling stories to one another from their holidays. I give them a group of words to choose from: 'luscious', 'obscure', 'hysterical', 'awkward' and they share vignettes from their holidays that are perfect examples. A lot of laughter and keen listening goes on as the stories flow. It's all about *human connection*.

Leaders can inspire and motivate their staff through storytelling. Everyday stories can link to something pertinent to a way of thinking you might like people to reflect on. A leader I was working with during a particularly difficult phase in her organisation began the workshop by recalling a time when one of her children became very ill while travelling overseas. She went on to talk about the reaction of all the people who knew her son. There were calls made to people nearby to visit him in hospital. Others in the country organised to be there when translation was needed. The leader telling the story was able to fly immediately to the area to bring him home, where friends and family had pitched in to look after children and pets and cook dinners. The son came home and was hospitalised for quite a long time.

As the story came to an end, the leader said to the quiet group: 'As I reflect on the path we are on at the moment, and how difficult it is right now, I think about the things that got me through that time with my son. It was the rallying of people who cared for us, who were prepared to put in because that is what you do when times are tough – you help each other be better than you were able to be by yourself.' The impact was immediate and heartfelt. The collaboration and honest conversation was due very much to the leader's courage and the story she chose to share.

I encourage you to build your storytelling skills. Schools are full of so many great stories that, when used with purpose, can bring out authentic dialogue and full engagement. *Hooked: How Leaders Connect, Engage and Inspire with Storytelling*, by two Melbourne thought leaders – Gabrielle Dolan and Yamini Naidu – is a great source of practical tips and tools to hone your storytelling skills.

Organisational Storytelling

One of my favourite collaborative question/listen processes for school teams is to have them tell the story of the school, either in small groups or as a whole team. People highlight the goals and strategies the school has been working on, the key events, people and achievements of the students, and the community involvement. These are captured visually on either A1- or A2-sized sheets for group work, or on a large, long chart on the wall. It is a very rich exercise, with people sharing perspectives and feelings. It weaves the tale of the school through dialogue and questions. The values of the school and the professional learning philosophy come to the surface, as do the key events and critical times in the journey of the school. I first came across this method from Grove Consulting in the United States. This global company uses visual strategy templates and high quality facilitation processes to help organisations identify their strategies for success.

I had the privilege of learning from the founder of Grove, David Sibbet, in 2014 in Berlin. For many years he worked in the corporate and not-for-profit worlds and is one of the most self-reflective people I have ever worked with. His teaching was peppered with insightful perspectives into how human beings work and how to frame collaborative discussions around possibility. Groves's term for the journey process, Graphic History, reminds us of the importance of all the steps in exploring hindsight, foresight and insight when planning for the future. Whenever I work with an organisation on strategy, we go to all three of these places and explore deeply to ensure we have had authentic conversations about what they tell us.

LEVEL UP – LET GO OF BEING RIGHT

Judith Glaser, the originator of Conversational Intelligence, has created a powerful way to look at the quality of our conversations. Based on research that looks at the brain responses to threat situations, the conversational intelligence model helps us to shift from conversations that confirm what we already know (Level 1) by talking about healthy and unhealthy conversations, how to communicate effectively and 'move people to a higher level of greatness'.

Her levels of communication are:

Level 1: Confirming what you know. Ask/Tell

Level 2: Defending what you know. Inquire/Advocate

Level 3: Exploring what you don't know. Share/Discover

To move up the levels we need to let go of being right and the conversations being 'all about me'. We also need to trust others and increase our willingness to be influenced by opinions and input. This framework supports the learning intelligence approach, which poses that congruent authentic dialogue is critical to building a strong collaborative learning culture, where co-creation and a 'we' approach are the drivers.

Glaser's book, *Conversational Intelligence*, is a must-read for those interested in serious self-reflection on your conversation style and its impact on your work and your life. It is full of useful and highly effective tips to help you identify your areas of strength and areas to develop. Conversational Intelligence has been built with the very latest research on how the way we hold conversations affects our brain chemistry and our threat responses.

WHAT'S IN IT FOR ME? ENGAGING PEOPLE IN DIALOGUE

No one needs to tell educators that life is busy. There are not many industries that can take the mantle from education of the 'Many Hats Award': teacher, academic, counsellor, family mediator, first aid expert, cyber safety leader, wellbeing advocate, subject specialist, pedagogical expert, administrator and collaborator! So we are pretty busy and there has to be a pretty good reason to listen. (Although in my experience teachers are a polite bunch of people who will give you a good go!)

Humans are driven by those things that motivate them. Of course, the trick is to identify and understand those things. Leaders who inspire and engage people, guiding their teams through a strong connection and an understanding of what inspires them, are definitely building the buzz.

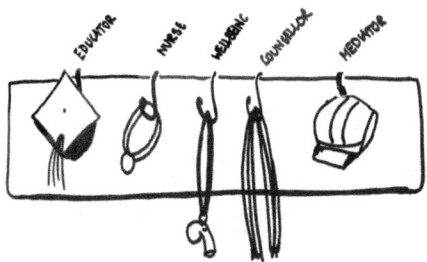

Teams that inspire each other ask questions that uncover how the team can work in a way that motivates and fulfills each person. Examples include:

Will [insert name here] help me to achieve a goal that I have?

Is this meaningful for the things I think are important?

Will this make my life and my work more:

- Interesting?
- Easy?
- Effective?
- Efficient?
- Engaging?
- Exciting?
- Fulfilling?

Will this make me a more effective teacher?

Think about the people in your professional learning teams – what motivates them? When you know this, you can engage people more thoroughly in conversations. Authentic dialogue is the key to these conversations – and knowing your people.

6. A FINAL REFLECTION

I couldn't finish this book without asking you to take a moment to ponder your current situation. Just as we hope that all educators take time to pause when exposed to new ways of working in the classroom, to reflect and plan how to trial or embed their learning, I would hope that we expect the same of ourselves.

My hope is that if you are reading this and you have a staff learning culture that doesn't have a buzz, or the learning intelligence is just not as sharp as it needs to be, you'll be inspired to take action.

Or perhaps the collaboration in your school is strong but could be pushed to even greater heights, to maximise the collective capacity and tap into the enormous talent, creativity and innovation in the individuals on staff? In this case I hope you have found value in *The Buzz* and will encourage and enable your high-performing team to strive further.

Our schools are full of positive and amazing educators, and many quality leaders who understand their role in focusing on the reason for their school's existence: the whole student and their learning. By building learning intelligence in your school you are arming all of your educators with the skills and beliefs that create a strong, cohesive and effective professional learning culture focused on growth and quality.

Figure 21 is a template for final reflections. I encourage you to take this template and sit down with a good glass of whatever refreshing liquid takes your fancy, either by yourself or with another person with whom you can discuss and explore your insights. Think with your mind, your heart and your gut about your vision for the learning intelligence in your school.

1. Vision

    - What would be apparent if learning intelligence were realised?
    - How would the buzz come to life?
    - Describe the mindsets and the dialogue.
    - What sort of compelling environment would you see?
    - What would people do and how would they feel?
    - Describe the impact on learning, on individual students and on the whole community?

Be specific. Look with optimism and possibility. Use bright colours and outcome statements that are in themselves compelling.

2. Present state

    - Identify the great aspects of your school

- *Identify those aspects that are not so wonderful.*

- *Use the lens of growth mindset, compelling environment and authentic dialogue to help you focus on the dance floor of your school. Use visual images and words to describe it. Be sure to include your own contributions so far.*

3. Craft your plan

    - *What will make the biggest difference in moving towards your desired state?*

    - *Who do you need to bring into the journey straight away?*

    - *What do you need to build or focus on first?*

These may be quite small steps or they may be big bold steps. The size of the step doesn't matter. Just make sure you identify those steps that will take you towards the buzz.

I wish you all the best for co-creating the buzz with your staff. I would love to hear your stories as you build your school's learning intelligence through:

- A growth mindset

- A compelling environment

- Authentic dialogue.

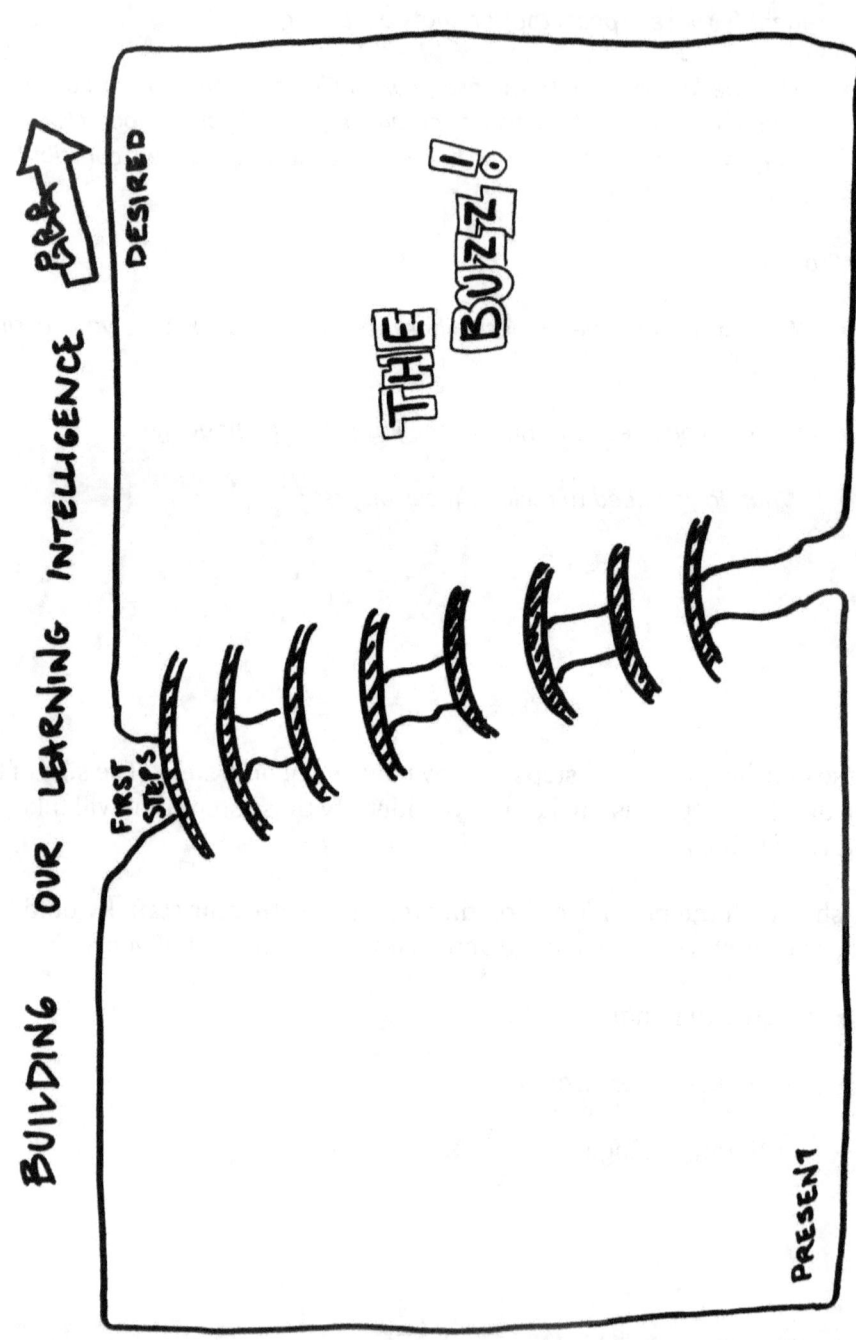

Figure 21 – Final Reflection

TRACEY'S PROFESSIONAL LEARNING BELIEFS

As educators we should be active, engaged learners.

Differing beliefs and perspectives give us great opportunities to learn.

Professional collegiate relationships are greatly enhanced when we believe we can learn from one another.

Every interaction is an opportunity to learn something if we wish.

Our beliefs are not permanent – at any time we can get more data (information, facts, emotions, perspectives) that can change a belief.

Deliberate curiosity is a foundational mindset of professional learning.

Everyone can develop skills, thinking, mindset, and attitudes.

As adults, our ability to see mistakes as learning opportunities has diminished over time.

As adults, we are pretty rubbish at being okay at making mistakes.

If we learn and apply continually, we develop a growth mindset as opposed to a fixed mindset.

It can be easier to sit in the comfort zone of our thinking.

Risk of failure can keep us in our comfort zone.

Collaborative professional learning and teamwork gives better outcomes for students and staff.

If we use collaborative tools with staff, we get better engagement and commitment.

Highly effective learners have a strong intrinsic motivation and internal locus of control.

Thriving learning environments are great places to hang out!

Seeing the possibility in things does not mean I don't know the challenges – I just seize the opportunity in them.

Cynicism is the enemy of growth.

Great teachers are as committed to their own learning as their students are to theirs.

Great schools are as committed to teachers' learning as to their students' learning.

SOURCES

Australian Institute of Teaching and School Leadership: aitsl.edu.au

Covey, Stephen 2004, *The 7 Habits of Highly Effective People*, Simon and Schuster, New York.

Dolan, Gabrielle & Naidu, Yamini 2013, *Hooked: How Leaders Connect, Engage and Inspire with Storytelling*, Wiley, New York.

Dweck, Carol 2012, *Mindset: How You Can Fulfil Your Potential*, Robinson, London.

DuFour, Richard 2007, 'Professional Learning Communities: A Bandwagon, an Idea Worth Considering, or Our Best Hope for High Levels of Learning', *Middle School Journal*, vol. 39, no.1.

DuFour, Richard; 2010, *Learning by Doing*, 2nd ed, Solution Tree, Bloomington

Fowler, Anthony 2015, *The Impact of Social and Human Resourcing Associated with the Curiosity and Powerful Learning Strategy (CPL) on Organisational Climate and Student Learning Outcomes at Warracknabeal Secondary College*,

Fried, Jason & Heinemeier Hansson, David 2010, *ReWork: Change the Way You Work Forever*, Vermilion, London.

Glaser, Judith 2013, *Conversational Intelligence, How Great Leaders Build Trust and Get Extraordinary Results*, Bibliomotion, Brookline.

Graham, Parry 2007, 'The role of conversation, contention, and commitment in a professional learning community', OpenStax CNX, cnx.org.

Hattie, John & Timperley, Helen 2007, 'The Power of Feedback', *Review of Educational Research*, vol. 39.

Hattie, John 2009, *Visible Learning*, Routledge, London.

Heifetz, Ronald & Linsky, Martin 2002, *Leadership On The Line: Staying Alive Through the Dangers of Leading*, Harvard Business Review Press, Boston.

Hemmings, Andrew 2013 'Talking Heads: How We Pulled our School out of Special Measures' *The Guardian*

McGeorge, Donna 2014, The Pen Is Mightier than the Slide, 2014, Donna McGeorge, Morrisville.

Medina, John 2014, Brain Rules: 12 Principles of Surviving and Thriving at Work, Home, and School, Scribe Publications, Melbourne.

Owen, Harrison 1997, Open Space Technology: A User's Guide, Berrett-Koehler, Oakland.

Robinson, Sir Ken 2010 'Changing the Education Paradigm' RSA Animate, thersa.org.

Rock, David 2008, 'SCARF: A Brain Based Mode for Collaborating with and Influencing Others', NeuroLeadership Journal, issue 1.

Rock, David 2009, Your Brain at Work: Strategies for Overcoming Distraction, Regaining Focus, and Working Smarter All Day Long, Harper Business, New York.

Sala, F 2004 'Just a Joke: Predicting Executives' Performance from Spontaneous Humor During Job Interviews', Hay Group, haygroup.com

Senge, Peter 1994, The Fifth Discipline Fieldbook: Strategies and Tools for Building A Learning Organisation, Nicholas Brierley, Finland

Sergiovanni, Thomas 2004, Strengthening the Heartbeat: Leading and Learning Together in Schools, Jossey Bass, New York.

Taylor, Carolyn 2005, Walking the Talk: Building a Culture for Success, Random House Business Books, London.

Timperley, Helen 2008, "Teacher Professional Learning and Development" The Educational Practices Series – 18, The International Academy of Education and International Bureau of Education, Brussels.

ACKNOWLEDGEMENTS

Appreciation and gratitude for this book being more than just a figment of my imagination go to a number of people. These people helped me persevere and also enjoy the process. They have helped me to see it as it is: a great learning journey and experience in itself.

To my family: Justin, my beautiful husband, for his unfailing support, love and patience, shown in so many ways, every day; Conor and Layla, who constantly fill me with joy, not only for who they are, but for showing me what a love of learning looks like. To Mum and Dad, Keith and Robyn Jessup, for putting in and supporting us as a family, and for always role modeling integrity and determination.

A special thank you to all the fabulous principals, system leaders, school leaders and staff I have worked with. I learn so much from seeing your high quality leadership in action and your commitment to education. Your input has made a huge impact on the contents of this book. A number of principals generously gave me their insights and time when I was testing out my thinking and asking numerous questions. Thank you especially to Kate Mitchell, Sharon Saitlik, Marg Pickburn, Lisa Yeoman, Jane Gibbs, Sue Dean, Mark Staker and Karen Patten. Thank you to Tony Fowler for sharing the work that he and his team undertook at Warracknabeal Secondary College. Thanks also to Dr. Briony Scott for allowing me to share her thinking on growth mindset.

A number of educators whom I greatly admire and respect took the time to give feedback on the manuscript. Their insights and feedback were incredibly useful and they have my deepest gratitude. Thank you Julie Symons, Coralee Pratt, Amy Holt. Thank you to my editor Ann Bolch for helping me shape this book into what you now hold in your hands. I loved our collaboration on this work.

To my professional tribe, all the Thought Leaders gang in Australia, led by the mighty Matt Church and Peter Cook – thank you for encouraging me to write this book and for providing great insights about how to approach it. To Donna McGeorge and Maree Burgess – you two are the best support crew and inspirers any woman could ask for!

ABOUT TRACEY EZARD

Tracey helps organisations thrive by focusing on building the key pillars of learning intelligence. The recipe for dynamic, forward momentum is: mindset, environment and dialogue. She builds the capacity of leaders and staff to create energy about their work and alignment on the future plans. She helps leaders and staff co-create and collaborate – and most importantly – act on their decisions! She brings these together in her first book, *The Buzz*.

Not afraid to discuss the tricky stuff, Tracey's background in education and her experience working with businesses in all sectors means that the things that need to be said get said and the things that need to be done are implemented. Her leadership development programs promote belief shift and resourceful mindsets that support transformation and momentum.

Tracey is well known for her high energy, interactive and engaging style. She uses visual tools to enhance the collaboration and 'stickiness' of the learning and affords leaders the momentum they need for improvement.

Tracey is a qualified educator and accredited in a number of tools, such as i4 Neuroleadership Assessment, Conversational Intelligence, Genos Emotional Intelligence, MBTI, Spiral Dynamics and Neuro-Linguistics Programming. She is a member of the Australian Council of Educational Leaders and the International Forum of Visual Practitioners.

www.traceyezard.com

www.ingramcontent.com/pod-product-compliance
Lightning Source LLC
Chambersburg PA
CBHW050318010526
44107CB00055B/2289